Thora Hird's
Book of Bygones

D1513839

Thora Hird's
Book of Bygones

Dame Thora Hird OBE

with Liz Barr

HarperCollins*Publishers*

HarperCollins*Publishers*
77–85 Fulham Palace Road, London w6 8jb

First published in Great Britain in 1998
by HarperCollins*Publishers*

3 5 7 9 10 8 6 4

A catalogue record for this book
is available from the British Library

ISBN 000 628068 4

Printed and bound in Great Britain by
Woolnough Bookbinding Ltd, Irthlingborough,
Northamptonshire

Contents

Introduction

I had just been speaking at a luncheon at an hotel in Park Lane, when it happened. A smart young man aged about twenty, accompanied by an equally smartly dressed young lady, approached me and said, 'Excuse me, Dame Thora, but what does that word you used just now – "*courting*" – mean?'

I said, '*Courting*?'

He said, 'Yes. In your speech just now, you mentioned the word "courting" and we were wondering what it meant.'

I said, 'You're not pulling my leg, are you?' and he said, 'No. We just want to know.' His girlfriend stood beside him, nodding perfectly seriously in agreement.

Now, this was no ignoramus. This was a well-educated, well-spoken young man. I said, 'Well, are you and this young lady going out together regularly?'

'Oh yes. We're getting engaged next year.'

'Well then, you've clicked... and now you're courting.' I don't think I left them very much the wiser.

When I was in the car going home, I began to think to myself, 'That word is dying. Isn't it sad for an intelligent young man like that never to have heard the word courting before, and not to even know what it means?' So I started thinking of words I hadn't heard lately... and so you might know, that's what this book is about. It's nearly a history book in its funny little way.

We know about all the wonderful, marvellous new things that have been invented during this century and are still being invented – things we would never have dreamed possible when I was growing up – but I don't think I had realized before how many familiar things were rapidly disappearing. I can remember so many words from when I was a child, words and expressions my mother used all the time, but it dawned on me, for the first time that day, that I haven't heard many of them for years. Words like mardy – 'Oh don't be so mardy!' if somebody's guerning – another good word. And kistey. If we left a bit of food on our plate, she would say, 'Oh don't be so kistey.'

Will there soon be nobody left who knows how to use a rubbing stone or a dolly-tub? How to black-lead a coal-hole or make a goose-grease vest? Play with a whip and top or dance the fox-trot?

It's a different world, but I hadn't noticed it altering. If you're as old as I am, I hope you'll enjoy being reminded of a bygone age, days of farthings and silver threepenny bits and florins, and that this little book will bring you a few happy memories. If you're still young, like the couple who set me off thinking about these things in the first place – please read on – this will be an education!

To show you just how different everything was in my young day, I have also included advertisements taken from a collection of contemporary weekly magazines and theatre programmes. I am confident they will astound you!

For starters, I am now looking at a programme
(price, 3d.) for:

**The Palace Theatre of Varieties for
Wednesday, May 20th 1908**

*(The Management politely request that where
necessary Ladies will remove their hats in
order not to obstruct the view of those sitting
behind. Gentlemen are requested not to
smoke at this Matinee.)*

After enjoying a bill that includes such
entertainments as:

The Bioscope

**Showing the World's Events from Day to Day,
including Types of British Battleships,
Whimsical People, Yachting in a Stiff Breeze
and The Naval Disaster in the Solent;**

---

with the top of the bill:

Miss Maud Allan,
presenting an extended repertoire of her Classical Dances, including "The Vision of Salome"

... and how would you like to enjoy a meal at a West End restaurant at these prices?

Pinoli's Restaurant,
(Under the personal supervision of the Proprietor, C. PINOLI),
17, WARDOUR STREET.
A SPECIAL 1/6 SUPPER FROM 9 TO 12.15 p.m.
Consisting of Soup, Fish, Entree or Poultry,
Vegetables, Ice, Cheese,
AND A
Special 2/- Parisian Dinner from 5 to 9 pm.

IDRIS
ROYAL TABLE WATERS
As supplied to H. M. the King

Chapter One
Washing Day

Do you know what a posser is? Do you know what a dolly-tub is? You've got them, you know, if you've got a washing machine. Nobody remembers the old names, but today's washing machines haven't got anything in them that wasn't being used when I was a child.

First, there was the rubbing board, or scouring or wash-board – many years later to be taken up and played as a musical instrument by the 'skiffle' groups in the 1950s. You had to soap all the garments and rub them hard up and down on the rubbing board to loosen the dirt. All this was done in the scullery (where you had your sink and dish rack for washing and drying the dishes, and where all the clothes washing was done). Then everything went into the dolly-tub, or sometimes

it was called a poss-tub, which was a wooden
barrel – like a beer barrel – held together with
iron rings.

The posser was like a long, sweeping-brush
handle, with a brass end in the shape of a
lampshade. You had to poss and poss and poss
the washing. My mother would put blankets or
bedding or heavy clothes in the dolly-tub, and she
used the same action as an automatic washing
machine of today... but in those days the
machinery was my mother and her strong arms,
using the posser to poss the clothes about in the
tub. I saw an old-fashioned posser quite recently,
hanging outside a hardware shop. I was never
more surprised to see anything in my life.

Then there was a dolly-stick, which you used
for hankies and socks and lighter things. It was
about a yard long, made of wood, and at the
bottom was a ring of wood and four rubber teats,
that looked just like a cow's udder. There was a
handle across the top, and you spun that round,
which was exactly the same action as today's
washing machines, whisking the clothes round
and round, and saving you from putting your

hands in the hot soapy water all the time. Then everything had to be swirled round in clean water, to rinse.

When you had done all that, the things were all passed through the mangle. Our mangle stood outside in the back yard, rather majestically really. It was made of iron, with two big wooden rollers. My brother or I, when we came home from school, turned a big iron wheel on the side, using a wooden handle, and my mother fed the clothes and blankets and sheets through the wooden rollers to squeeze the water out.

(Of course, another thing that lived in the yard in those days was the toilet. You had to cut up old newspapers and thread them on a string for the outdoor loo. When you were in there, you'd get a bit and start reading it, and then you couldn't find the continuation. My mother used to call out, 'You can stop reading – I've washed up!')

Another thing that lived very near to the mangle, in the part of the yard we called the wash-house, was a stone boiler. Underneath was a little grate in which my father built a fire, using wood and coal. A large copper receptacle was embedded in the stonework and filled with water, and a generous sprinkling of Hudson's dried powdered soap. Then the sheets and bed-clothes were put in to boil. It was lovely and warm and steamy out there in the back yard on a cold Lancashire winter's morning. You can still see them nowadays, the old coppers... usually polished up and filled with logs in country houses!

The work that was put in, every Monday! My mother did all the big, heavy stuff in the morning, and then hung them out with dolly pegs – clothes pegs to you – in the yard to dry and air. The line was then raised by a clothes prop – a long pole with a V cut in the top to lift the washing line high in the air. Blankets did not have to be washed every week of course, but the bedding was, all the sheets, valances and pillow-cases. You don't often see valances nowadays do you? We always had them. My mother used to make them. They were usually made of white linen, with a draw thread worked in, pulled up to make a frill, and they were fastened all round the bottom of the bed by a tape. They hid the gozunder!

Your carpets had to be taken up and steam-cleaned, and beaten, to get all the dust out. Sometimes a steam-cleaning van would come round to the house, and you could take your carpets out to them.

Being washing day, Monday was the day we just had mashed potato with whatever cold meat was left over from the Sunday roast, because that was an easy dinner on a busy day – just a big pan of potatoes (kept in a wooden box under the sink) salted and mashed with freshly churned butter bought from the milkman.

After the clothes had been boil washed, put through the mangle, and dried on the line, items like sheets and towels were brought back into the house and hung over a clothes rack or clothes horse to air.

One morning, I was at the front of the house scrubbing the steps – which was rather like being in an armchair receiving people, because anybody passing would always stop to have a few words with you while you were there. At the top of Cheapside was a corner shop, with one window in Cheapside, and one in Market Street, and it was part of the entrance to the theatre. There were three floors above it with rented out rooms – one was to a Mr Withers, a sign-writer, who had a notice: 'I made signs before I could talk!' I always thought it was very clever, that.

On this particular day, Mr Withers was passing by. He always walked with a tilt, like Jacques Tati's Monsieur Hulot, and wore plus twos, not plus fours. Plus fours and plus twos were gentleman's breeches, wide at the top, buttoning up under the knee. Plus fours were baggier than plus twos. He said, 'Good morning, Thora.'

'Good morning, Mr Withers.'

Very polite, you see, the conversation.

Then he said, 'I take it your mother doesn't object to you putting your hands in a bucket of diluted dog-shit?'

And I tittered, because he had said 'shit' – *nobody* used words like that in those days... and I was only eight. I said, 'Oh no, Mr Withers.'

'No. I see. Well, good day to you.' And off he went.

I ran inside immediately, to ask my mother what 'diluted' meant.

This was how I learned about words – asking my mum or my dad on the spot. My mother was wearing her cleaning apron. (The cleaning aprons were grey, and cost tenpence each.) She had just lowered the clothes rack down and was shaking the damp towels and putting them out over the rack to dry and air. She said, 'What is it?'

'What does "diluted" mean?'

She said, 'Diluted? Oh well, let me think how I can explain that to you. Well. You know when I ask you to go and get sixpenny worth of lime, down at the woodyard?'

I said, 'Yes.'

She said, 'Well, then your father adds water to the lime block – that's diluting it – thinning it with water, so he can whitewash the yard walls.'

The clothes rack was pulled up and down by a rope on the wall, with a double hook, called a cleat, that you wrapped the rope round, in a figure of eight. Everybody had one. She had put the last towel on, and was starting to pull the rope to take it up, when she said, 'What did you want to know for?'

7

'Because Mr Withers said that he takes it you don't mind my putting my hands in a bucket of *diluted* dog-shit.'

Zoom! The clothes rack rocketed up to the top so fast it banged the ceiling! She'd pulled so hard, the thing nearly went through to the bedroom above. She said, 'He *what*?!'

I said, 'He said he takes it that you don't mind...'

'Oh did he? Well never mind that – go and get the steps finished.' And I could hear her muttering to herself, 'I shall have a word with Mr Withers... speaking to a child like that!'

When my mother was ironing, in the kitchen, she would always sing.

O where is my boy tonight?
Oh where is my boy tonight?
My heart overflows for I love him, he knows.
Oh where is my boy tonight?

I'd sometimes accompany her on the piano, Neville joining in on the violin. Another favourite was, '*Sweet violets, sweeter than all the roses...*'

Ironed handkerchiefs were always folded into squares and put onto a dinner plate on a shelf over the fireplace to air – it looked exactly like a plate of sandwiches. I can see her now, folding up her ironing sheet, singing away in the warm kitchen. The ironing sheet was for putting over the kitchen table – no fold-away ironing boards for us.

The flat-iron my mother used was a bit smaller than a modern steam iron. I've still got it, my mother's old iron. A lot of things that were once ordinary household objects are now being collected and sought after as decorative items. I've put my mother's old iron on the window ledge in the cottage, because I've recently had it hand-painted with daisies and poppies. A neighbour of ours in Sussex, Daphne, always has very imaginative ideas. I was round for coffee and I saw that she'd got an old cobbler's iron last, but she'd had it painted by a bargee she knows who is also an artist. So you might know – I've had him do it for me too. As well as my mother's old

flat-iron, he painted for me a shoe last that was
my father's, which I use for a doorstop, and an
old-fashioned jug that was originally plain white
enamel, with a blue rim. Everyone remarks on
how beautiful they look.

I didn't have a washing machine when I was first
married, in 1936, when Scottie and I moved in to
our own little house, Prompt Corner. I used to do
all my washing by hand, or in a dolly-tub, and
hang it out on the line before I went off to
rehearse on a Monday morning; the train drivers
used to lean out of their cabs and wave at me as
they passed, while I was hanging out my two long
lines in the garden – particularly once Jan came
along, when there was always a long row of white
terry towelling nappies. No disposables in those
days!

    I got my first washing machine after the war,
when we were living in London, a twin-tub – and
now that's already almost as old-fashioned as a
dolly-tub!

'"Cantilever Pressure" they say! A good job of work is what they mean...'

'Cantilever pressure! Something like the Forth Bridge, the man in the showroom said. This is how *I* found out. I wanted to know whether an ACME could do a full family wash – including the blankets – and still come up smiling and not leave me fagged out. Now I know. It *does* take blankets. It *is* easy to turn. It *does* store easily out of the way. And it does *not* squeeze the middle and leave the edges still wet – that's 'cantilever pressure'. The main point is that instead of having a heavy ugly machine taking up half the kitchen when it isn't in use and terribly backaching to turn, I've a first-class wringer-mangle which does all I ask of it in half the time, and when it isn't wanted it goes to bed out of the way in the kitchen cupboard. You can believe me, to do a good job of wringing you need an ACME.'

Chapter Two

A Well Regulated Household

Let us suppose that you said to a child of ten, these days, 'Would you go and fetch me a gas mantle?' They wouldn't know what you were talking about, would they? Whereas, when I was a child, gas mantles, the fourpenny sort, provided all the light for our kitchen. Or you could get an inverted mantle – for sevenpence. I can remember that to light it, you pulled a little chain down to release the gas and then, with a taper, you lit it through the little hole in the middle of the glass bowl that went under the mantle, being very careful not to touch the actual mantle, because it would disintegrate the minute you did. Whenever you were putting a new one in, your parents would say, 'Now just be careful with that mantle!'

Ours was a well regulated household. We had a crocodile's leg and foot, with little claws on, hanging on the front of the hearth, on the left. That was for the tapers – strips of newspaper, rolled round a knitting needle, then you pulled out the needle and turned in the ends, and stored the long thin tapers you'd made inside the crocodile's leg. You could also buy white wax tapers, if you were a bit posh. Most people made their own, with newspaper twisted round a knitting needle.

When you think of all the things a newspaper came in for in those days – apart from reading the news I mean! For the yard toilet, you cut it up in squares, eight inches by six, and threaded them on string; you rolled it up for your tapers to light the fires, or – very carefully – to light the gas mantle; you put it down on the floor when you had scrubbed it and had done the yellow-stone, to stop people walking on it when it wasn't quite dry, because you didn't want them walking the yellow-stone through the house. 'Now don't you walk on my nice clean floor!' Who gets down on their hands and knees these days, to scrub and put yellow-stone on their kitchen floor?

It's where I got the idea from for Edie, in *Summer Wine*. People stop me in the street and say, 'Ee, when you put those newspapers down – it does take me back. My mother always used to do that!'

Where we do the filming for *Last of the Summer Wine*, just on the next corner to the cafe are the biggest windows for a hardware shop you ever saw, which amazes me in a little town like Holmfirth. They have all sorts of old-fashioned things – brass coal scuttles with little shovels, stone jars, and enamel jugs. Can you remember those cans, white with a navy blue edge, and pale green with a darker green edge, enamel cans, with an enamel cup on top, attached with a wire?

All the men had them, who took their lunch to work, with a 'twist' of tea, it was called. A little bit of tea in a screw of paper. And people took them on holiday. In all the windows in Cheapside there used to be signs: 'Tea brewed here. Tea, coffee, or hot water.'

It was threepence for someone who had come along with one of those cans, and a twist of tea, and you brewed it for them. Then they took it

back to the sands. And if they hadn't one of those
things, you charged them sixpence on the jug –
and of course they brought your jug back to get
their sixpence back. Cheapside was near the
sands, so someone – the mother as a rule – would
come up from the beach, with their can and the
twist of tea, and you brewed the tea for her; or
else she paid sixpence deposit for the jug, and
brought it back. If you lent them cups, it would
be a penny, and over the summer season, it
mounted up.

Eleanor Woodhouse, the Andersons, Grandma
Woodhouse, Lena Maxwell, the Edmondsons –
they all made many a shilling brewing tea, and
saved them in an empty cocoa tin.

My mother didn't have a sign, but she 'took in'
summer visitors – three shillings a night, during
the season – to get the money together for the
rates, eight pounds a year. It wasn't easy money.
Fresh sheets had to be put on each time, all
boiled, aired and ironed. She would never charge
her visitors for a cup of tea or coffee at night,
before they went up to bed, and she never
charged them for 'the cruet'. The cruet might be

a jar of vinegar, and a salt and pepper pot. A lot of seaside landladies charged their visitors twopence for night-time drinks, and threepence a meal for 'the cruet'. They put all those coppers into an empty cocoa tin, and it went towards their own holidays. You can't blame them. I used to ask my mother why she didn't charge for more things, but she'd always say, 'Well, they've come here for years – the Longs from Leeds. Their Albert and their Winnie. I couldn't charge them.' They would come every year, some families. For their dinner, they would provide the meat and my mother would cook it for them. On a Sunday, you might have the Long family's roast of lamb, the 'girl and her mother's' two chops, and our own family joint. I've often seen my mother do four different lots of meat on a Sunday. You sold them potatoes and vegetables, although as a rule they brought their own, and you didn't charge them anything for cooking them.

Which has taken us a long way from the workmen's tea cans. Last time I was in Holmfirth, I saw some of them in this big hardware shop. I just had to have one. I said to Jan, 'You think I'm daft, don't you?' She said, 'I don't. I know exactly where you'll put it. You'll put it in the cottage next to the sink, where you can see it and remember the old days.'

There was another thing that went on in our street in the winter. I can guarantee, you could go down and see in every window – at Eleanor Woodhouse's, the Newbys, Grandma Woodhouse, the Maxwells, the Armstrongs, the Brayshaws – always, every winter evening, a big frame over their knees, sitting in front of their fire, pegging a rug. They'd ask you for any old clothes, trousers or suiting. These were cut into three- or four-inch strips. They each had a wooden peg their husbands would make for them, with a pointed end. A piece of canvas was tacked on a frame, you made a hole and used your peg to push the pieces of cloth through, and then you turned it over, and you had a rug. They looked so nice, but I'm here to tell you were the best dust catchers ever invented. Because when you took them out into the back yard to shake them, you needed a gas mask. You'd throw them away after a bit.

Outdoor loos

Ours was a proper water closet. It flushed. In some parts it's called a Petty if there's no flush. Then the night soil men had to come in the night to collect the waste. That's why there were little doors in back streets, next to the back gate, a little door, with a little fastener, where they opened up the back of the loo and put a shovel in to collect the soil. What a job, eh? They'd have a horse and cart at the bottom of the lane. There have been a lot of improvements, haven't there? Not everything was good about the good old days.

You had to keep an outdoor privy spotlessly clean. Izal in the water, scrub the floor, and yellow-stone it. It was a Palace of Varieties, with all the different acts you had to perform to keep it clean. There was no varnish left on the seat, it had been scrubbed so hard by my mother.

Home decorating

Those were the days of aspidistras on the sideboard, and antimacassars – usually white lacy cotton squares thrown over the backs of chairs

and sofas, they were there to keep the grease from
the men's hair-oil (Macassar) off your furniture,
but they were pretty and decorative as well. We
also had an artistic Cornish frill in our house.
For anyone who is not *au fait* with what a
Cornish frill is, it was a frill that hung from the
mantelpiece, either pinned on, or threaded on a
string and tied round, like a little curtain, and it
was the same colour as the curtains and cushions.
The magic was, I could go to school, leaving the
room lilac coloured, and come home to rose pink.
My mother had done her routine: curtains and
Cornish frill down, cushion covers off, all washed,
dyed (with a fourpenny drummer dye), dried,
ironed, aired... Everything back up.

And for a week or two you'd be in a different
coloured room, until she changed it all again.

Our walls were done with distemper, or colour
wash, as it was sometimes called. Our upstairs
walls were painted pale green or pale blue, and
the ceilings were white. You couldn't wash the
walls, if there were greasy finger marks, because
if you did, you washed all the colour off, so we
always had a bucket of distemper handy to cover

over any marks, and the whole house got a fresh coat once a year.

The bedroom door in the front bedroom had four panels, each one painted with different flowers: irises in one, poppies in another, cornflowers in another, daisies – marguerites we called them – in the other. It was like that when we first moved in – some artistic previous tenant had done it. I loved them. Every year, all through my childhood, my mother used to say, 'I think we'll paint those panels over this year.' I used to plead with her, on behalf of these things, 'Oh leave them!' And they were still there when I left home to be married.

Once I was engaged to be married to Scottie, I loved getting things for our new home. Every bride-to-be in those days would have a 'treasure chest' or 'bottom drawer' in which to collect things gradually for her new home. Woolworth's were doing a new line of kitchen utensils, for threepence and sixpence, the handles were all in green with a white line round. I wanted a green and white kitchen, so whenever I had a little money saved up from my one pound a week working in rep., I'd go and buy a few, and collect them in my 'treasure chest'.

Our bedroom was painted in a pale green wash, and I made our bedside tables from empty boxes I got from the Co-op. On one side we had a round drum of three-ply that had once been full of desiccated coconut. I scrubbed it out and painted it in green to match my chest of drawers, that I'd also painted green. And for the other side of the bed I found a miniature tea chest, the same height, that had been full of ground almonds. They made lovely little bedside tables. I put a pair of book-ends, holding three books, on one. I don't think I ever read them – I just thought they looked good. We had no light upstairs, only candles, so you each had a candlestick beside you, on your bedside table. And my mother gave me a green bed cover. It all looked so nice, and cost us next to nothing.

I must have been mad on green at that time – my kitchen was all done in green and white, too. I was the first person I knew to have a coloured gas stove. It was the only one they had at the gas show-rooms, and it was pale green, so I bought it.

Thora's antiques roadshow

But although so many things have disappeared, of course there are a lot of people – me for instance! – who like to keep them, however old-fashioned. For instance, do you remember butcher's wooden skewers? I remember saying to Ernie Brown, the butcher, when a new batch came in, 'Save us one or two of those, will you?'

He said, 'Aye, well, you do right, because now they're sending us steel ones with a loop on the top.' I've kept a couple of the wooden ones in a drawer, scrubbed and wrapped up in tissue paper, all these years.

You don't always notice little things like that going. Milk bottles, for instance, I'm sure will soon be a thing of the past – they're nearly all plastic now. I'm holding onto a couple of glass ones. Before long, mark my words, it will be smart to have flowers arranged in an old-fashioned glass milk bottle – people won't have seen one for years!

Which has just given me an idea for something else which you never see now – stone hot-water bottles. Wouldn't one of those look lovely with marigolds in? I've got one that I use as a door-stop, but it's just struck me how nice it would look on the kitchen table with marigolds in it.

Although it takes a lot of cleaning and polish-ing, I've always loved brass, and I've got quite a few old pieces at home, every one with some memory. I've got a pair of brass candlesticks that were my father's grandmother's, my great grand-mother's and, as I tell Daisy, her great-great-great grandmother's... and there isn't a scratch on them. I have two sets of brass weights to remind me of when I worked at the Co-op – not that I need reminding, it was such a happy time. Eight pounds, seven pounds, six pounds, four pounds, two pounds, and one pound. I keep them on a ledge in the stairway in my London home.

Scottie bought me a tea-set when I was in *Maid of the Mountains* and he was in the orchestra. A tea-pot, milk jug and sugar bowl, with matching cups and saucers. Very worn and used now – but nothing would buy those from me. They hold such memories as you use them.

What else? I still have my old school slate, with a wooden border, and a piece of chalk. The actual one I had at school. It's very useful. I keep it near the kitchen door and I write on it the things I've got to remember the next day – things I need to take with me to rehearsal and so forth.

I've got two or three of the big stone jars, with a brown varnished rim, that had seven pounds of marmalade in them. My mother used them for storing pickled onions and red cabbage. And I'm still using my mother's old round wooden bread board.

Coal-holes and chimney pots

What else did we use for the housework then that you don't use now? Black lead. That's something I *don't* miss. You had to put this solid lump of black stuff in a saucer, mix it with water to the consistency of a paste, and then rub it on the fire grate and the coal-hole lid. It was horrible, messy stuff. When Zebo came out, in a tin, oh boy, were you somebody if you had that! I took ours outside to do the coal-hole lid, and left the Zebo tin lying about ostentatiously, so the neighbours could see what I was using.

You don't even have coal-holes any more do you? With coal-hole lids? Going under the house?

I don't suppose many households have any use for Zebo, either. It's all central heating these days.

When Jan and William lived at the Mill House, where Scottie and I had had our cottage in the grounds of their estate, we had five Victorian chimneys in the garden, that Christopher Beeney gave me, from his mother's old house in Hastings. We had nasturtiums growing out of them. Sadly, when Jan and William sold the place, they left them behind. I didn't notice for ages, and then it was too late. I'm still mad about that.

Not in my life-time, but it wouldn't surprise me if one day you hardly ever saw a chimney pot. It will all be central heating. You'll only see them on very old houses... or in people's gardens with nasturtiums growing out of them!

Chapter Three
The Ghost of Christmas Past

I have gone on pilgrimage three times now; I have twice been to Bethlehem and seen where Jesus was born, but I have never been there on Christmas Day. I'd like to do that one year – if I'm spared! (That's another expression you don't often hear now, isn't it? 'If I'm spared!')

When I was a child the celebration of Christmas never began until after work on Christmas Eve; and, unlike now, everyone went back to work on the day after Boxing Day... but our *preparations* for Christmas began long before.

First, four Christmas cakes were baked at the end of September. You kept the cakes, wrapped in greaseproof paper or a damp cloth, inside a tin. In those days, as I've mentioned, butcher's skewers

were wooden, not metal. My mother would scrub
one of those clean and then use it to pierce the
cakes in a different place each week, adding a
tiny drop of brandy into the hole, just about a
teaspoon, once a week until Christmas. Ooh,
those cakes were delicious. You only had a tiny
bit at a time, because they were so rich, and some
people managed to keep one cake back until the
following Easter. People would come to our house
for tea on a Sunday, and tea in those days meant a
knife and fork do, with a bit of fresh Lune salmon,
from the River Lune, four miles away, and then
my mother would say, 'Would you like a bit
of cake?'

'Ooh yes please.' I'm afraid ours never lasted
until Easter.

The second stage of the build-up for Christmas
was 'mincemeat Sunday'. It was always the same
week in November. 'Now don't be making any
arrangements for Sunday, because we'll be doing
the mincemeat,' my mother would say. (It was
always 'doing the mincemeat' not 'making the
mincemeat'.) You bought a lump of suet from the
butcher's – you didn't get the fine shredded suet

you buy in handy boxes now – there was none of
that. You grated it yourself.

The worst part of mincemeat Sunday was
doing the raisins. There was none of your
Sherwood's seedless raisins then. Our Nev and I
would have a little knife each – 'Go and scrub
your hands and under your nails first' – and we'd
cut the seeds out. Can you think of anything
more boring? You didn't have to do it with the
currants, just the sultanas and big raisins. By
golly, that was enough. It took hours and we got
so fed up. Nobody was more delighted when
Sherwood's brought out stoned raisins. I bought a
packet immediately, although I didn't want them
for anything. Just to look at it – stoned raisins.

The mincemeat was made in the bowl part of a
'toilet set'. (That's a big porcelain jug and a bowl,
and a complete one also had a long dish for your
toothbrush, about ten inches long, a smaller soap
dish, all in the same china or porcelain, and two
'gozunders' – what 'goes under' the bed! I've still
got a gozunder, one that my grandmother had,
white, with a three-inch turquoise stripe round it.
I put bulbs in it for spring.)

All the currants, sultanas, raisins, candied orange and lemon peel cut in thin strips, suet, allspice, grated apple and probably a lot of other things which I can't now remember, were all stirred up together in the large toilet-set bowl, a clean tea-towel was put over the top, and then it was left in the pantry to settle for a couple of days.

You would put the first lot of mince into one of those seven-pound stone jars, the kind with a brown varnished rim, that everyone keeps their wooden kitchen spoons and things in nowadays, and you made a lid with a bit of boiled white rag. Then the one-pound jam jars that the rest of the mince was going in were washed and warmed. I don't know why they had to be warmed. We filled about twenty one-pound jars, and you could buy little transparent papers that went directly on top of the mince – I never knew what they were for, but you always did – and then you cut out circles of greaseproof paper to go over the top and tied them round with string, to make a lid.

*

Nearer to Christmas my mother would make the pastry for the mince pies. I remember she always made a hole in the top to let the steam out with a sterilized darning needle – and where would you find one of those now? Who darns these days? Nobody.

That mincemeat was so good, it was worth all the trouble in the end. You didn't make a dozen mince pies for Christmas, you made about a hundred, because everyone who called, friends and neighbours, carol singers, all got a glass of ginger wine and a mince pie. We had to have so many one-pound jars of mincemeat, because whenever anybody said, 'Oh, that was a lovely mince pie!' my mother would say, 'Oh, do have a jar!' She was always giving away stuff that we'd worked hours on! I used to think, 'Don't be so generous!'

While we're on about mince pies – at the school party we had plates of them, and any mince pies with three air-holes instead of one had a silver threepenny bit in them. (I didn't discover this important information until after I'd left, unfortunately!) On the plate there would only be

two mince pies with the silver threepenny bit in,
all the rest had nothing. Do you remember the
tiny little silver threepenny bits?

The lights in the Co-op, where I worked after
leaving school, were an electric bulb and a white
opaque shade, about the size of a dinner plate.
They put a coloured serviette over the shade at
Christmas, with the four points, to make it
look gay.

At home, we put holly behind all the picture
frames in the kitchen. And it was the only time
that things were 'allowed' on top of the piano.
My dad would never permit anything on top of
the piano as a rule, not to be disagreeable, but
he took music very seriously, and he thought an
instrument should be treated with respect. But
at Christmas he allowed a glass dish of Turkish
delight, walnuts in another dish, and chocolates
in another.

On Christmas Eve, when it was dark, we lit the
candles on the tree. The wax candles were wedged
into little tin holders, shaped like a star with four
little points that you squeezed inwards to hold the

candle, and a little presser clip to go round the branch of the tree. Of course, with the candle, it was heavier than the branch, so unless you put it almost in the middle of the tree, it would begin to droop, but you tolerated that. We had them for years. And we always had a fairy on top of the tree, with a little tissue paper dress.

It was a lot of work, all this pleasure! The tree with the candles that clipped on, and were always falling off, was put in the front window. 'Don't get it too near the net curtains!' Your mother or father always had to sit near it when the candles were lit, to make sure the curtains didn't catch fire. But four o'clock in the afternoon of Christmas Eve in Cheapside, when darkness fell, when you saw all the trees lit up by candlelight in all the windows along the street, that was always, for me, the most magical moment of Christmas.

My father would be home late, coming off the pier, on Christmas Eve, because he would call in at Houghton's for a box of tangerines and a pineapple. The box would be 14 inches square, and the tangerines in each corner would be wrapped in silver paper.

He also used to call at Charlie Howe's Music
Shop, on Queen's Street. Charlie Howe sold
pianos, instruments, sheet music and records,
and my father always brought home ten new 78s
– records for the wind-up gramophone – as his
contribution to the Christmas season.

My Auntie Clara always sent me a cake of pale
green toilet soap, glycerine and cucumber, which
my mother put in the toe of my stocking.
Anything small, like a lace hankie, would go
in the bottom.

Neville always got things to add to his Meccano
set for Christmas. Nowadays there are such
wonderful things for kids, but in those days
Meccano was a real novelty, because you could
make something that really worked. There were
little screws with square bits that went on the end,
and tiny screwdrivers. They were beautiful things.
Every lad had Meccano in those days. Your father
bought you the number one, number two,
number three – whichever you hadn't got. One
year Neville got one that made a steam engine, so
that when the wheel went round it moved along.
And my father would help him to build it – never

mind breakfast, they just wanted to get down to building the Meccano.

In our house Father Christmas used to come down the chimney into the front bedroom. The parcels always had a sprinkling of soot on, that's how we knew. Once there was a huge parcel that had come down the bedroom chimney – so big it couldn't have come down the chimney, but you didn't think of that. It was all magic anyway. And there it was, in the front bedroom, with rain and soot on it, 'Open Sesame – Love from Father Christmas.' It was a beautiful, hand-made, miniature billiard table. I learned to play billiards on that.

At four o'clock on Christmas morning you were up! One year I woke up at three, to see our Neville sitting on the end of his bed with a black sou'wester and an oilskin mac on that Father Christmas had brought him, dressed up like a Skippers sardine tin. My oilskins were yellow. When it rained in Morecambe, being on the sea-front, it really came pouring down. When you came indoors, you stood and a little lake would form around you, with all the water dripping off your oilskins.

I can see Neville now, wearing all this, three o'clock in the morning, sitting at the bottom of the bed, opening his other presents. 'Now go back to bed!' a sleepy voice would call from my parents' room. 'You can open your other things in the morning.' But no fear. No fear.

Chapter Four

Have You Heard
the Muffin Man?

They didn't come from Charles Dickens' famous
United Metropolitan Improved Hot Muffin and
Crumpet Baking and Punctual Delivery Company,
as described in *Nicholas Nickleby*, but we did have
exceedingly good muffins, delivered to our door.
Mr Slinger was our muffin man. I can see him
now, in a sports jacket and cap, carrying a great
big butcher's basket, covered with a spotlessly
clean linen cloth. He sold muffins, crumpets – or
pikelets – milk-cakes and a large, flat, ready-made
pancake, nearly the size of a place mat, which you
could toast. Scottie used to tell me how in
Staffordshire, when he was a lad, they would make
oat-cakes that size, and when it was cooked you
rolled it up round a sausage, and ate it like you do
a hot-dog.

Mr Slinger would be round to our front door every Monday, Wednesday and Friday afternoon, so the muffins went straight onto the toasting fork for tea. A lot of them were still warm from him baking them, at his home.

And it wasn't just muffin men who walked the streets of our cities, towns and villages in those days. Nearly all the tradesmen used to come delivering to your door. Like the watercress man. He was a little cripple, and he cried out 'water-cre-e-ess' with a little yodel. He'd picked it that day, and it was in an old basket on his back, with the water still dripping out of it. You'd go with a dinner plate to the door to get a pennyworth. You'd get a mountain of fresh wet watercress for that.

His daughter used to come round midweek with mushrooms, fresh picked, for fourpence for half a pound. You can't believe it, can you?

At night a man used to come round with a little machine with two wheels on, nearly like a milk-churn, but not as deep, with hot peas in. He used to shout, 'Hot peas! Peas – all hot!' but it used to sound like 'Peas a lot!' because an aitch was never near it. You went outside with your basin for a pennyworth.

They could all be pretty certain of lots of custom, because their things were so fresh.

And the fishman – Gil Johnson in our case – with his little horse pulling a flat cart covered with a spotless linen bedsheet. We were four miles from the Lune, so my mother always got a piece of Lune salmon on a Saturday when he came round, and she would cook it for Sunday tea. In those days kippers were three halfpence a pair. There's another thing. You don't really go for a *pair* of kippers these days, do you? At Blackpool, you could go to Fleetwood, where they sold you a wooden box of Fleetwood kippers. Each box would hold two pairs, that was four kippers, and you could send them off as a present. Every time I did a season in Blackpool I must have sent off at least a dozen boxes of Fleetwood kippers – to my cousins in Manchester and people like that, because these were the best, freshest kippers you could imagine. What a lovely breakfast, fresh kippers with brown bread.

Harry Mabson would come to the door selling

bundles of firewood for three halfpence a bundle.
You still see bundles of firewood these days –
they're always the same shape – but his had just a
suggestion of the smell of tar. He used to chop the
wood at home, and then dip the ends in a little
tar to help them burn, and then sell them door to
door, although later, when I worked at the Co-op,
we used to buy the bundles of firewood wholesale
from him, and sell them in the shop.

Another commodity that came to the door was
lamp oil. It was a foreign gentleman, round our
way, and he used to call out as he walked along –
it sounded like 'Blake Oil!' – selling oil for your
lamps. He also sold rubbing stones, or donkey
stones we sometimes called them, for rubbing on
the steps. A penny they were. We always got them
from him.

A rag-and-bone man would come round, with
a hand-cart, with two handles. All round the end
of his cart were little windmills made of sticks, as
long as knitting needles, and a piece of wallpaper
folded into four points, and fastened with a
drawing pin. They would be whizzing round, and
children would pester their mothers to give him

some rags, or buy something from him, so that he would give them a windmill. He only gave them to the kids whose parents did business with him. They didn't last long, but they were a great prize.

The milk was always brought in churns on a milk-cart, straight from Thornton's Farm. Ernie Thornton would come in the house, and with a tin measure that hung on the side of the churn, he measured out a pint, and we put it in a pot jug. And we got our butter from him, just a piece of paper underneath and up the sides, and with a little pattern on the butter on top. But ooh, lovely butter.

Our greengrocer actually called round to the house to take our order. Watesons had a son and daughter, and they would come round on a Saturday morning, knock, knock, and you gave them your order. 'Right. Two pounds of sprouts, six pounds of potatoes, what have you got fresh this week? Have you got any... so and so?' And May Wateson would write all this down in *our* notebook, the one they kept for our orders, and you paid when the stuff came, about two hours later. Sometimes Jimmy Nuttall used to come with the delivery – he worked for them. He always talked for so long, having his cup of tea, my mother used to say, 'Let's hope you don't stay everywhere as long as you stay here, Jimmy, or you'll never get through!'

I have written before about the 'cut apples'. Houghtons had a fruit shop and a butcher's shop, side by side, and if you took along your mother's enamel bucket full of potato peelings, they took it out the back and fed the peelings to their pigs. Then Billy Hadwin, the boy who worked at Houghtons, would say, 'Will you have a cut apple or a banana?' The cut apple was like a piece of sculpture – they'd cut out all the brown bits, so there it was with holes all round it; or you had a black banana that you couldn't peel, it was so over-ripe. At home we had our own fruit dish on the table with beautifully washed and polished apples and pears – but I had to get a cut apple, the same as Clara Woodhouse and the others!

The butcher didn't deliver, but the grocers, Simpsons, would always deliver large orders. My mother became a Co-op member later on, but I'm speaking about when I was a very little girl.

Simpsons put a great big wire pedestal, like
Blackpool Tower, at the door of the shop, with
fresh eggs in it; but they had to take it in,
eventually, because nearly every dog that passed
helped himself to an egg. It's true! I saw it
happen. Those were the days when, if you asked
what the cheese was like, they would give you a
bit on a knife edge, to try. My brother was such a
cheese lover, he would always want to be the one
to go to Simpsons for any errands, so he could
do a bit of sampling.

I remember Kraft cheese coming out – I hope
Kraft cheese aren't listening or reading this book,
because my mother said it was just like soap.
I didn't think so, I loved it. It was about a foot
long, but square, like a long cube, with silver
paper round it, and they'd slice you some off.
I loved it. I used to pinch a bit to eat on the way
home, if I was collecting it.

Then there was the knife-grinder. He had a
machine rather like a sewing machine he used to
push down the road. It had a grinding-wheel that
he worked with a treadle, and he sharpened your
carving knives for about a penny or twopence.

The only time I can remember actually seeing him at work was when he sharpened a big pair of scissors for us, the ones we used for cutting cardboard.

I think it might have been the same man who did the chair bottoms. I know he used a sharp knife. Most people would have bentwood chairs with plaited cane bottoms. He'd repair them, sitting outside in the street, cutting off new bits of cane and plaiting them in.

Then my brother Neville got a job at Sheppertons, the wireless shop. They gave him a bicycle with a big box on the front of it, and he had to go to people's homes, collect their wireless accumulator, take it down to Sheppertons, where they'd charge it up, and then deliver it back.

Who else came to the door? Lamp lighters, for the gas lamps, with the long pole and a little chain they pulled down, the same action as we used indoors for the lamps in the kitchen. In some places, like mining towns, where most people had to get up very early, the lamp lighters would also be 'window tappers' or 'knockers up'. When they came to put out the lamps in the early morning,

they would tap on your window to tell you it was
time to get up.

We had a gas lamp right opposite our front
door. It had a big hook, that flopped down when
they pulled it and the light went on. The first time
they did me on *This is Your Life*, they had got that
actual lamp from the Morecambe Corporation.
It was standing on the stage at Shepherd's Bush
with artificial snow falling on it, like a scene from
Dickens. The very one that I'd played marbles
underneath, all those years ago, and so many
other street games.

OLDHAM ACCUMULATORS

"– not only has this accumulator an **INSURED LIFE** –
but it will definitely give you *ninety hours* of Wireless
without recharging"

"– *ninety hours, eh? – why, that's over three weeks!*"

"Yes Sir, it's a bit different from the old days when they
used to run down once a week."

"*Why, that'll save me quite a bit of money in the long run.*"

Types and Prices
Oldham O.25 ... 5/-
Oldham O.50 ... 9/-
Oldham Plus 124 ... 14/9

Chapter Five

Old-fashioned Remedies

I was in the company of somebody recently who
said they had a goose every Christmas, but had
never saved the grease. 'Ah well!' I said, 'We
always did.'

You saved it in a jar. It was a ritual in winter in
Morecambe. The smell isn't very nice and, in class
at school in winter, you could hardly bear the
stink! Your mother rubbed your chest and
between your shoulder blades, and made you what
was called a 'front', like a little vest, out of brown
paper. She would cut straps, and it was pinned
together with a gilt safety pin. You put your arm
through one strap, and the other was wrapped
round and pinned on, to stop the goose grease
going on your vest. Mother would cut about a
dozen, and you put a clean one on each morning

in the cold weather. It was supposed to stop coughs in the winter, and was also good for chilblains.

When Jimmy joined the RAF, they were rifle bashing in Skegness, and he got chilblains on his poor musician's hands. He wrote to their Rita to see if she had any goose grease, and she sent him a jar.

Living at the seaside, because of the cold wind off the sea, we would often get a bit of a chest cough or a cold in winter. Some people had camphor bags. A camphor block is like a mint, and your mother made a little silk or satin bag for it, out of a bit of hair-ribbon, and you hung it round your neck. You could breathe more easily. How I longed for one of those! Dorothy Burrell had one. Pink satin hair-ribbon with a little corded edge. I kept putting on a big sniff, and saying I thought I had a cold coming, but my mother would say, 'Well you're not having a camphor bag. You're putting it on.'

If she thought I was genuinely suffering, she might say, 'Well go along to Whiteheads and get six pennyworth of oil of almonds and essence of violets.' It came in a little glass phial with a cork in. It was a beautiful pansy-purple colour, you had a teaspoonful and it was a lovely syrup. People were known to put a cough on, so they could get 'six pennyworth', because it tasted so nice. If you were badly bunged up with cold, you had a bit put up your nose on cotton wool.

They sold sixpenny phials of perfume at Whiteheads – in a little basket on the counter – Californian Poppy and Shemin nessim, and little threepenny cakes of soap.

My hair was washed with carbolic soap, and a bit of borax in the last rinse. What that did, I don't know. Then I'd sit on the fender to dry it over the fire – it's a wonder I didn't catch light.

They also sold worm cake at Whiteheads – which looked exactly like Liquorice Allsorts, the ones with pink and blue spots on – which you had as an anthelmintic. (You don't want to know what that means.) And they sold fly papers – the 'fly cemetery' we called them. You could buy sheets of sticky paper, and you hung them on the light in the pantry, or wherever food was kept, and flies would get stuck to them. Butchers always had them. They were horrible, with little black bodies stuck all over them. And jam jars full of water with a bit of jam floating on it, full of dead wasps.

The sign outside an old fashioned chemist's shop would be a pestle and mortar. Women would go in to Timothy Whites or Taylors for a discreet brown paper parcel of 'towels'. If you were 'lying in' – that is having your baby at home – the District Nurse would be in attendance every day, often for as long as a month. It was a much riskier business then, having a baby, than it is now.

Chapter Six
Playing in the Street

For the last fifty years – more – I have lived in a cobbled London mews. I love the cobbles. It's an art, cobbling. It used to be so beautiful – each cobble stone perfectly matching the ones either side, and raised in the middle, so the rain drained off them. People kept hens out on the front in the old days. But once they started taking the cobbles up to lay down mains water, gas and electricity, and then telephone and television cables, for every five they took up they put three back. And once they started, they came and took them up and laid them down again so often, they lost a lot of the regular beauty they once had.

They were taking some of them up again only last week, because of a gas leak. The noise was terrible. They put the cobbles back disgustingly, but a few days later a proper cobbler came and put them all back more artistically. It will never be as good as it was when we first came, but at least there are still a few people left who take a pride in doing things properly. The old arts and customs are dying. Things like cobbling, tiling, thatching, or building flintstone walls. Jan and William live in a Sussex Queen Anne house, all flintstone on the surface, and along the lane, their high surrounding wall is covered in flints. It's beautiful, and I don't know how they managed to cut them in half so exactly that they are all matching perfectly, all the same size, and all done without the aid of any of the wonders of modern science.

Another thing that is now forgotten, nearly, is 'playing in the street'. In Cheapside there were a lot of other children, and we all knew so many games. Like hopscotch, on the Yorkshire flags – even though we were in Lancashire! As a rule, up to ten flags along was as far as we went. I've always thought of myself as a bit artistic and neat, so I used to like chalking the numbers, one to ten, on the flags. (After you'd finished playing, your mothers always made sure you cleaned the chalk off the pavement.)

It was supposed to be the one who first got her stone or slate into each of the squares, and hopped in and retrieved it successfully, who was the winner – but we all made up our own rules. If things weren't going your way you'd change the rules, 'Oh yes it *is* fair!' The battles there were!

We had different street games for different times of the year. At Easter – I don't know why – we always played battledore and shuttlecock. A 'battledore' was like a small tennis racquet. A feathered shuttlecock would be twopence – a cork base with feathers glued all round it. A whip and top was another Easter game – a wooden top, costing about a halfpenny, and you had a whip, with a lash made of string. You coloured your top with rings of different coloured chalk, so that as it spun round it changed colour. You could be very artful with a whip and top – you could keep it going for half an hour if you were skilful at it. You wrapped the string of the whip round and round the top and then pulled it, and that started it spinning. Then you whipped it to keep it going.

In the summer, there was swimming. We loved to go in at night, a whole gang of us, and my mother would let us have the back bedroom to dry off, and she would have big jugs of cocoa ready downstairs. She used to say, 'All I will say is that every other night you will sweep that room out.' Because it would be full of sand. We were like fish, living by the sea, in and out of the water all summer.

In the winter – well, it was twopence each to go to the cinema on a Saturday, to see Pearl White or Dr Fumanchu. I was always Pearl White at home, left tied to the railway line with a train coming, as you left the cinema. But you knew she'd get off in time.

We had a couch at home, horsehair, with big arms, which were our horses – because Nev and I were Tom and Mary Whitfield, cowboys. I can never remember where we got those names from.

After school, we used to play round the clock tower, near the Children's Corner – that was the name of a corner on the sands, where there were four very big steps, flat steps four inches deep that we used to run down. The fishermen's landing stages had every third wood taken out during the winter, because of the storms, to let the sea through, so the landing wouldn't be washed away.

The fishermen would come ashore with a stringful of flukes (dabs some people call them, but we didn't) – about three or four inches long. They'd say, 'Do you want a stringful of flukes, joy?' – 'joy' was what they called you in Morecambe, not 'love' or 'darling'. And you went home and your mother would say, 'Oh don't bring any more! I've got a back yard full!' These were baby plaice, with the red spots on, the freshest plaice you could ever imagine! I could easily eat four for my tea. As you took a forkful off the backbone – that was all there was. It was like eating satin – for nothing.

Ethel Armstrong and her brother lived on Renshaw Street, in Manchester. They were my playmates whenever I was staying with my Auntie Nellie on Rossermund Street. We played out in the street, even in Manchester. Ethel's father was a

tailor, so when we were playing hopscotch she
would borrow his piece of marking chalk – do
you remember tailors' three-sided marking chalk,
for marking the material, before they cut it out?
It was perfect for hopscotch. But he was mad,
because once we wore one out and he hadn't
any left.

Auntie Nellie would let us play in the cellar,
where we would play 'shop' – all little girls love
doing that. In her cellar Auntie Nellie had the first
mangle I had ever seen with rollers made of
rubber. We used it for the till. We used ribbon
paper – if you went to buy a yard of ribbon,
there would be paper underneath – and we
put it through the rubber mangle, like a cash
machine.

Back on Cheapside, Spi's ball was a game we all
played – but we always pronounced it Piesball –
for two or more players. It was our version of
rounders. You ran from one 'hob' to another.
There would usually be no more than six hobs,
which you marked in the street – so in our case,
one was under the dressing room window, at the
Royalty; number two was on the lamp, across the

road; number three was near a gate, further down... and so on. One person would throw the ball at you, and you hit it with your hand – no bat or anything – and then you ran from one marked 'hob' to the next, while the bowler retrieved the ball and tried to hit you with it while you were running between different hobs. It was safe to play and run about in the road because in Cheapside the most hectic traffic were the occasional horse trams, on their way to Lancaster. One of the tram stops was right outside the theatre, which meant there was always plenty of horse manure in our street, which my mother would send me out to collect in a bucket. I often wondered how our plants survived – there was more horse manure on them than there was soil – and some of them grew very, very tall and thin, and I always swore it was so they could get out of reach of the pong!

I bought a secondhand push-bike for half a crown, a Rudge Whitworth. I got a sixpenny tin of black enamel from Woolworth's, to paint it over, but because I never rubbed the old enamel off, it looked like a bike with varicose veins. I used

to go riding along with a tennis racquet balanced
on the handlebars, and a net with four tennis
balls in – I didn't play tennis, but I thought it
looked 'well off'. What a swank! And whenever
I could borrow Lena Hacket's bike – which was
a new one – I would, just to ride it round the
streets, to show off.

Another game we enjoyed – which we
sometimes got into trouble for – was 'Follow my
leader'. Two of you set off with a piece of chalk,
while the others turned their backs and counted a
hundred with their eyes shut (if they played fair).
Off you'd go, and you'd make little chalk arrows
on the various gate-posts that you passed. There
was a little woodyard in the street, where we
bought wood for the boiler in the yard, and the
blocks of lime for whitewashing the yard walls,
and that was usually the first gate that we marked.
They used to shout out at us, 'Now you're going
to come back and clean that off...!' And finally
you found a place to hide. It was as simple as that
– the rest of the gang had to follow the arrows
until they found where you were hiding. So
simple – but such fun!

We had competitions, for who was 'best'. A
thing we all had, boys and girls, was a bowler – a
ring or hoop of wood, which you hit with a little
wooden stick – and then you ran the length of the
street bowling your ring along. It was good
exercise. A boy would usually have an iron or steel
one, and the stick that he hit it with was somehow
linked with a ring onto his bowler. I'm probably
not explaining this very well.

Then there was skipping – now that was a
competition. The most usual game was, you took
it in turns holding and turning the ends of the
rope – which was a good long one. Then everyone
else, one by one, would run into it as it was turning
– towards you, never away from you. That would
have tripped you up. And there was a thing we
said – 'Pitch... patch... pepper' – you went into
the rope and as you jumped you went 'pitch'
(hopping on the first foot), 'patch' (hopping on
your other foot), 'pepper' landing on both feet,
and then you went on jumping with both feet,
everyone counting your jumps and you trying to
keep the pepper on longer than anyone else – and
then you ran out, and someone else would run in

and go 'Pitch... patch... pepper... one, two, three, four...' until they ran out of steam. Of course, you nearly died trying to keep going longer than anyone else.

There were lots of games, that we made up. Another one was jumping over the rope, seeing who could jump the highest. We didn't jump the way they do for the high-jump today, in the Olympics. We jumped one foot after the other in front of us, and if you were very clever you turned in mid-air, as you jumped over, so you landed facing the other way – then everyone would applaud. Clara Woodhouse was good at that.

We used a bit of rope from an orange box, or from an onion crate, which were the same – made from plaited raffia. We'd go along to the greengrocers, Houghtons, and say, 'Have you any orange box rope?' They'd be throwing it away, so they didn't mind giving it to us, so the supply was unlimited and completely free. That's so different from nowadays.

Pip, Squeak and Wilfred were cartoons in a newspaper. You could join the Pip, Squeak and

Wilfred Club. Ick ick, par boo, goo goo par nunk – that was the password, if you read the strip.

The most expensive luxury item we ever had was when the first unburstable 'Saw' balls came out. An ordinary ball cost about 3d., and these cost one and six at Paynes, the cycle shop. We all gathered outside Mr Payne's shop, and stood in contemplation. When he first got them there were six in a box, on display in the window, dark green and dark blue, and the 'Saw' ball design printed on them. They were solid rubber balls, so they couldn't burst – this was the joy. Most of us saved up – you usually got threepence a week pocket money, or if you nagged your parents enough, you might get given one. The game with the 'Saw' balls was to get them to bounce from the ground to the wall, back to the ground, and to turn round before you caught it. The game, again, was who could keep going the longest without dropping it, or missing the bounce.

I was never the best in the street at that, by any manner of means, but I think I was probably one of the best at skipping. At the school sports day I was always picked for the hundred yards. I couldn't run a yard further than that. We had sack races. Egg and spoon races. There was so much excitement about it all. And yet nearly everything we played with was absolutely free, or just a few coppers.

As I'm writing this a friend of mine has just come in, because he has been out to buy a skateboard for his nephew for Christmas – *eighty* pounds... Bloomin' 'eck!

Chapter Seven
Sheet Music

We had a sheet music shop on the central pier at
Morecambe. After I had left school at Whitsuntide
I had been so sad, standing in the window
watching my friends going up the street back to
school, that my mother had said, 'Get your school
bag and go and ask Miss Nelson if you can stay for
another term.' I had been back for about three
weeks, when one day my father arrived at the
school's top door and Miss Nelson called me out
of my place and said, 'You can go with your father.
He's found you a very nice job at the music shop
on the central pier.' The shop was run by Arthur
Hickman-Smith, and it sold all the latest sheet
music. In the summer the piano was pushed out
into the doorway during the day, and a little easel
was set up on top of the piano with a copy of the

music and the notice, 'This week's popular number now being played.'

My job was to play the piano and serve the sheet music. I didn't sing. They never made the public put up with that! I could play anything in two sharps or three flats – after that I was finished. I remember one I liked playing was called *Dearie*.

> *Dearie, you are my Dearie.*
> *I want you every day...*
> *And when I feel you near me,*
> *All my world seems bright and gay*
> Diddle-dee, diddle dee...
> (That's the piano part.)

Meanwhile, at the far end of the pier, at the outdoor ballroom, they'd be playing the latest popular music there as well, and people would come along to buy the sheet music of whatever they had been enjoying dancing to, so they could have it at home. The dancing outside on the pier started at about ten thirty in the morning – with a big band on the bandstand. The Miss Hintons' cafe was just there, so you could go in for a lemonade, or a cream soda. It finished at about half past four, because the dancing was indoors at night, in the big ballroom.

I'm knee-deep in daisies was very popular. I can still remember it, after all these years:

> *I've just had a bonny letter*
> *from a pal who went away.*
> *He's on a short vacation,*
> *a little recreation.*
> *Guess my pal is feeling better,*
> *here is what he's got to say,*
> *'No I won't come back, no I won't come back,*
> *I'm down here to stay – I'm knee-deep in daisies,*
> *and I'm head over heels in love...'*

We couldn't wrap 'em up quick enough!

You wrapped up a sheet of music in a piece of tissue paper and left one end to tuck in, and not the other. 'Sixpence, thank you.' People would buy them and learn the words and play them at home. They might have been fox-trotting with someone on the pier, and it brought back

memories when they got home to Wigan –
especially if they'd fallen in love on their holidays,
which nearly everyone did.

The songs really moved people. Years later, when I
was doing a season at Blackpool, I met Lawrence
Wright, who wrote many of the old songs, but by
then he was in a Bath-chair. Lawrence Wright or
Horatio Nichols – he published under both
names – I don't know which was his real one.
He was a millionaire when he died, and he left
everything to his secretary. They'd met when she
had been a piano player at the sheet music hall he
had in Blackpool. She invited Scottie and me for
lunch once, at his house up on the North Shore.
After lunch she sat down at the grand piano and
said to us, 'Do you remember this one?

'There's nothing left for me
of days that used to be,
there's just a memory
among my souvenirs.
Some letters tied with blue;
a photograph or two;

I see a rose from you
among my souvenirs.
A few more tokens rest
inside my treasure chest,
but though they do their best
to give me consolation,
I count them all apart
and as the teardrops start
I find a broken heart among my souvenirs.'

He wrote that one, and I'll never forget seeing her
there at the piano, playing it, singing it... and she
was crying.

There was a lot of singing for pleasure in those
days. Our piano was in the kitchen at home. I've
already said how in Cheapside lots of people took
visitors in, during the season, and on a Sunday
morning you'd hear all the pianos going and
people singing popular songs – not many hymns,
I'm afraid. You kept the music in the seat of the
piano stool, but also inside an empty orange box.
Orange boxes were just wooden crates, made
from slats fastened together, with two partitions,

but if you stood them up on one end, they were just the right size and people used them for keeping by the piano for all the sheet music. We had one – wallpapered to match the kitchen!

The music would often have a picture of a well-known singer or actor on the front. I remember *Among My Souvenirs* and *Maid of the Mountains* had Josie Collins on the front, because she played in *Maid of the Mountains*. *Dearie, You are My Dearie* had Ernest Binns on the front, who was the nephew of the men who owned the pier.

We also had another big stage trunkful of old sheet music at home. When my mother went into the business, because as a girl she'd sung *I Know that My Redeemer Liveth* for years at the local church, the minister and the congregation had bought her this trunk as a going away gift. It was big, with a dome top, made of leather, and it was full of sheet music from my mother and father's period, when they had been 'in the business'. Music with Little Titch on the front, and The Chocolate Coloured Coon – Elliot – and people like that.

On a Sunday night our house was never without callers, who would be 'just passing' and come in for a drink, and there would be singing. One famous song my mother had sung in her professional days was *The Gift*, a song about a baby.

> *'What shall I give to thy Child?', he said,*
> *softly caressing the sleeper's head.*

It's Jesus talking to the mother. The child's dead, I think. I used to go through to the back kitchen, weeping, and my mother would come after me and say, 'Come back in the other room.' I'd say, 'Oh please don't sing *The Gift* again!' It was her big success, but I didn't like it. It upset me too much.

The jazz bands were the pop stars of our day. We weren't quite as potty as the kids are who go to an Oasis concert or whatever today – but in a way we must have been nearly as mad about it. Apart from the ballroom dancing, the sheet music and sing-songs, of course, we had our wind-up **gramophones, and played and danced at home to** all the latest 78s. They got scratched very easily, and you had to keep changing the steel needles, which you kept in a small His Master's Voice tin, but we thought they were wonderful.

I remember one we had by the Camptown Strutters Band, a marvellous tap-dancing tune Nev and I were mad about. Another one was:

Hard Hearted Hannah,
the vamp of Savannah,
the meanest girl in town!
Leather is tough, but Hannah's heart is tougher.
She's the kind of girl that likes to see men suffer!

I think we had eight different records of that. One was a sixpenny one from Woolworth's. We put it on over and over again. We played it so often my mother said, 'If you put the other side on, you'll still get *Hard Hearted Hannah*, because you must have played right through it with the needle!'

Chapter Eight
Seaside Holidays

I don't want to be the mayor of Morecambe, but I wish I had been given five years to be in charge of keeping it how it was – a fishing village – instead of trying to be like Blackpool.

How can a village compete with a big town, and what is more, the top seaside resort in England? But there was always this, 'Well, we're just as good as Blackpool!' Of course we weren't as good as Blackpool. Our illuminations were little candles in jam jars, lit by volunteers. But I stuck up for it when I was there. We would say, 'Oh, I think these are nicer than Blackpool...' Nicer than Blackpool! It was pathetic.

But it really was lovely when there were the sailing boats, and the old fishing families would take people out on boat trips. Willacy is a great

Morecambe fishing family name. There were
uncles, cousins, dozens of branches of the same
family. The Willacys and Woodhouses. They were
sprawling families – every street would have a
Willacy or a Woodhouse in it. Or a Mayor – my
mother's father, my grandad. I wish I'd known
him. He was a character. He used to stand on the
top of the landing, in the summer, when they
were taking visitors for sails in the fishing boats.
He'd say, 'Now then, yadies' – he said 'yadies'
because he couldn't say his Ls – or his Rs or his
Fs – properly. 'Now then, yadies, any mair goin'
yowin', shaiyin' or shishin'?' Meaning – any more
for rowing, sailing or fishing. You'd see them
come in, with two fish on the end of a bit of
string, to take back to their landlady to cook.
You can imagine somebody on holiday, say from
a mill town, catching a fish, and while they're
eating it, thinking, 'I caught this!' It was a real
achievement. It was something they never
forgot.

The shrimp fishing industry in Morecambe in
those days was very important. The trawlers had
no engines or anything, they were just little boats,

but there were a lot of them, and a lot of families
depended on the fishing. The shrimps were grey
when they were caught, and the fishermen's wives
would boil them in the boiler in their back yard.
Then they would 'pick' them – never 'shell', we
said 'pick' – and take them in calico rag bags
down to sell. Then the Co-operative Fishermen
started, when the 'rough' shrimps – with their
shells on – were delivered to the Fishermen's
Co-op, where the women would collect them,
take them home and pick them and then take
them back again. People had a picking table. They
would rest their elbows on the low table, squeeze
out the head, take the tail off and flick it, so they
had a pile of shells and a pile of shrimps. We had
one in our cellar, but we only picked for our own
use. My mother always bought them 'rough' and
then we picked them at home. My mother was
like a machine, she was so fast – she had done it
as a little girl, a fisherman's daughter, before she
could go out to play.

The measure was a mullinger – rough shrimps
were so much a mullinger. The mullinger was like
a big pewter mug, and that was piled high. You'd

go to the fish market, and ask for a couple of mullingers of fresh shrimps.

People on holiday took bags of shrimps in their shells back home as presents. Shrimps and Morecambe rock were the most popular things you could take. You can still get this delicious delicacy – Morecambe Shrimps – sent to you from Baxter's in Morecambe. The Mr Baxter who sends them – I remember his father so well. One of the smartest men I've ever seen. Beautiful blazer, a good fit, black and white check cap, a handsome man, and when I was fifteen or sixteen, I was madly in love with him – but he never noticed me.

'Hallo, Harry!' I would say, hopefully.

'Hallo, Thora, how are you?' But he never noticed me. I used to think, 'Oh you are so handsome!'

All the fishermen trawled for shrimps, and they were sold all over the world – well, all over England, anyway. And the importance you felt, if you stood by while they were loading up crates to put on the train, and you saw 'London', 'Birmingham', and you'd think, 'Ooh! Morecambe shrimps!'

I remember when we first moved south to live in London, happening to pass a shop, Young's, and seeing in the window nothing but piles and piles of different sized pots of 'Morecambe Bay Potted Shrimps'. They were a great luxury in those days. I could have stood there for half an hour, just looking at the words, Young's Morecambe Bay Potted Shrimps.

The fishermen all wore navy blue ganzies – not jerseys – ganzies. Oh, the smell of boiling shrimps in all the back yard boilers, at night, in the summer! You'd take a deep breath, and my mother would say, 'Oh dear! They're boiling shrimps in Sun Street!'

'A fish and two' was a great expression. We bought them at Robin's Fish and Chip shop. It had a highish counter with vinegar and salt on it, in case you were going to eat them on your way home, and a large notice up which said, 'Keep smiling! It's your turn next.' A fish and two was what eight customers out of ten would order – a fish was threepence and you had two pennyworth of chips. And we would say, 'Put a few crimps on' – that was the little bits of crispy batter that were loose. They were lovely. Fivepence bought Nev and me many a supper. Half of the fish each and half of the chips. Then it got very fashionable to have a big potato, sliced, dipped in batter, two pieces, usually oval, and a bit of fish in the middle, then put in the fat. Scallops, we called them. Twopence each, they were. Sometimes we'd have one each, Nev and I.

With Morecambe being near the Lake District, we could go to lots of events like Grasmere Sports. All the places round about had their sports days. You'd say, 'Are you going to Cartmel this year?' You had to go on a bus to that. You went with your sandwiches. There would be three-legged races and egg and spoon. You can't think what excitement there can be had, running with an egg on a spoon. 'Are you going in for the egg and spoon race? Well he won it last year. You won it last year, didn't you, Clifford? He won it last year.'

There was a hound trail – owners with their dogs following an aniseed trail. One man would have gone for a long walk before it started –

several miles – with a bit of rag smelling of
aniseed on a piece of string, and then the hounds
dragged their owners along, following the smell
of the aniseed. Not all the dogs were hounds –
anyone could enter. It was a big annual event.
I can see it now, written up in chalk on the board,
'Grasmere Hound Trail'. The men who organized
it were all very self-important, 'Well, I'm on the
committee this year, you know, for the Hound
Trail...' Just about pulling a bit of smelly rag
across the countryside!

And then there was a paper-chase for the men,
running across country in their shorts – really just
a refinement of our 'Follow your leader' but when
the first man came in, you take it from me,
no-one has got cheered like that! 'He's 'ere!
He's 'ere! Hoora-a-ay!'

You spent the year preparing for these things.
We had Morecambe Carnival Procession –
even while they were in one procession people
would be saying to one another, 'Next year he's
going as Oliver Cromwell.' Because they were
preparing for the next one as soon as one
had started.

Why was it so short a time ago – and it is a short time, as old as I am – that there was full enjoyment from such simple pleasures?

What sums up the charm of Morecambe for me is when my father was in charge of the pier, and there was a room at the end where the deck-chairs were kept. Not a room – a shed. They were put away in there at night, and my father used to go in every morning and not let them put out any chair that had a dirty mark. They were kept clean, or he threw out any that were badly worn or couldn't be cleaned. He'd say, 'No-one wants to pay threepence to get their dress dirty.' There was such a lot of thought that went into everything, to make it pleasant. I think that would describe Morecambe. It was threepence to go on the pier, where there was a bandstand and outside dancing – you didn't pay extra for that – and you had a clean deck-chair. It was wonderful value. Then there were all the little shops and places you could get a coffee, or be weighed, or have your photo taken.

Our season wasn't as long as Blackpool. They had the brilliant idea of having the illuminations

in the autumn. The London Midland and
Scottish Railway put on special trains to 'Go and
see the Blackpool Illuminations.' A big name
switched them on. 'George Formby will be here
to switch on the Illuminations.' Solid thousands
would be on the promenade. I've seen this, season
after season. They couldn't see him, but they
cheered.

They were on until after midnight. You could
get six in a cab if you pushed in. The cab-drivers
made money, and the men selling hats with 'Not
Until After Seven O'Clock George' and all that on
the front. Everyone was making money at
Blackpool. The fish and chip shops. When you
went on the promenade with your kids, you paid
to go into the Tower, paid for the Menagerie, for
the Zoo... Dancing was an extra sixpence – Reg
Dixon on the organ in the morning, and they
would all be there dancing, '*Oh I do like to be
beside the seaside*' – half of them in curl pins. They
wore them all day – coloured curl pins – knowing
that the time for 'clicking' was at night. 'Clicking'
– that's another word, but it's one for the next
chapter…

Then there was Lobby Ludd. Was it the *Daily Mail* or the *News Chronicle*? You had to have one folded up under your arm and go up to him and say, 'You are Mr Lobby Ludd. I claim the News Chronicle prize.' You'd win a fiver.

Meanwhile – back in the ballroom on the central pier, Morecambe – we used to have the Daily Sketch Spot Dance. The lime perches, on the pier, were in boxes. Neville was often the boy on the perch, swivelling the lights round the ballroom while everyone kept on dancing, and whoever the limelight was on when the music stopped won the Spot Dance prize. Some people would waltz round very fast, trying to chase the light round the floor. There were some wonderful prizes, like a canteen of cutlery – but the man had to have the *Daily Sketch* in his pocket to win it.

When he started work on the central pier at Morecambe, my father had had the big concert hall turned into a beautiful ballroom. It had a big dance floor, with a fountain and greenery in the middle. All round the side were seats that had been in the auditorium when it had been a theatre. You could have a good night out. It was the first ballroom in England to have non-stop dancing. Jimmy Little's band at one end, Benny Bolton's at the other. As Benny Bolton finished his set with '*Oh horsy, keep your tail up, da de dum de...*' at the other end Jimmy Little, in the same key, would pick up the tempo and before Benny Bolton had finished his band would be playing: '*... da de dum de... Does... the... spearmint lose its flavour...*' So you could dance on.

Midland Railway

The best route for comfortable travel and picturesque scenery to the holiday resorts.

Peak of Derbyshire
Yorkshire Inland Spas
Morecambe and the Lake District
Isle of Man
North of Ireland
All parts of Scotland

Send a postcard to any Midland District Station Master stating where you wish to travel and information guides will be forwarded by return.
Derby 1907   W. Guy Granet
                                        General Manager

Chapter Nine
Courting

Courting – the very word that started me off thinking about all these things, because of the young couple who didn't know what it meant. I suppose originally it comes from the idea of 'paying court' to a king or a queen, but in Lancashire, by the time I was old enough to be doing it, in the 1920s and 30s, it had come to be how you described a couple who were serious about each other, and were just about to become engaged to be married – they were courting. 'Are you courting?' meant had you got a very serious boyfriend.

Courting was just before the engagement, when you became 'the intended'. 'Is this your intended?' Or 'Have you met my intended?'

Of course, you had to go through a lot of other stages before you were courting, or became 'the intended'.

The whole thing might start on a dance floor or at a party, or even on holiday, when you 'clicked'.

What was clicking? Supposing that you are two girls walking along the promenade at Morecambe, and two boys are walking the other way, and they like the look of you, and turn and follow you, well, you have 'clicked'. It was almost like a formal game. There was no fear, like now. You were aching for them to follow you.

'Excuse me... Are you on your holidays?' This was from two yards behind you. If it was on a Monday, the big holiday romance had started, because you were there all week. There were more broken hearts on a Friday night in Morecambe and Blackpool than you've read about in the Brontës. Having a last kiss, he would say, 'I'll write to you...' Not often, but sometimes, a correspondence really would begin, and they would both try to arrange their holidays – or most probably it would be their parents' holidays – so they could meet again for the same week the following year... and there could be plenty of Darby and Joans reading this book today who first met when they 'clicked' on Morecambe promenade.

You clicked. If you then found you still liked one another, on better acquaintance, after two waltzes, say, then you would start 'walking out'; if all went well, you would then say you were 'going out regular'.

'Are you going out regular with anyone?' That was what Jimmy asked me, standing in a bus-shelter out of the wind on the front at Morecambe, so I could tie my head scarf, the very first time we had gone out together. And if I had said 'yes', he probably wouldn't have asked me to go out with him again.

You were a flirt, if you walked out with lots of different boys. I'm afraid, until Jimmy came along and I knew he really was the one I didn't want to get away, I did go out with different boys – but just for fun. A lot of girls took this all very seriously. I thought it was a bit boring. If they were 'walking out' with one boy, they would never go out with another, even though walking out was far less serious than courting, or even than 'going out regular'.

Ballroom dancing was very popular at that time, and when visitors came to Morecambe for their seaside holiday – it was very easy for us local girls to click, if we wanted to. You would go on the pier, to the big ballroom, and there would be all these young fellows on their holidays. If they asked you for a dance, and your steps rather fitted in with theirs, they would ask you for the next one. That didn't necessarily mean you'd clicked – just that you liked dancing together. The fact that someone could do a new step in the fox-trot was much more important than whether he was good looking or not. There were some very good ballroom dancers in those days – boys as well as girls. We were all taught ballroom dancing at school. And we were taught that it was for the boy to go up to a girl and say, 'Please may I have the pleasure of this dance?' And after it was over, they would take you back to your friends. You can see that happening now, can't you? With Oasis playing on the stage?

Most of the young fellows were good dancers – looking very smart in their holiday best plus fours. During the week many of them would come in to buy cigarettes or something at the Co-op, and they could see me at the cash desk. I used to duck down and hide, if I saw them first, because I would have told them I was on my holidays from Bradford or somewhere. My girlfriends and I used to have a meeting on a Monday night to decide where we would 'be from' that week. 'Let's be from Barrow-in-Furness.' It was silly really, but we felt we weren't as interesting if they knew that we lived in the place.

But supposing you had clicked. Then, if you were dancing at the outside ballroom, they might buy you a Horlicks or a lemonade – threepence – in the cafe. It was usually a Horlicks you'd have, as you sat along the pier. It's hard to explain to today's young people that that was our idea of fun – ballroom dancing and drinking Horlicks. But it was fun. We thought we were so sophisticated, but when I think of it, looking back, we really weren't. We all thought we were the Clara Bows of Morecambe, real heartbreakers, but we weren't.

It was a very good way of getting to know people, dancing. There was no harm in it, you weren't afraid a boy would attack you on the dance floor. It would seem now that everything was so simple that gave such a lot of enjoyment.

'I'm happy when I'm hiking...'

I've a picture at home, of me sitting on a five-barred gate, with short skirt and the brogues and the earphone plaits. While a lot of clicking, walking out, seeing someone regular, and even courting, took place at the pier ballroom, Scottie's and mine didn't. We didn't go dancing together. In spite of a good sense of rhythm, from being a drummer, dancing wasn't his best thing.

We had 'clicked' on our second meeting, at a party where they were playing 'Postman's Knock'. You play it like this: somebody goes out of the room, knocks on the door and says, 'Post!' The door is opened, they say who the letter is for: if a girl is the postman she will name a boy, and if the boy is the postman, he will name a girl. The one whose name is called goes outside, the door is shut, they kiss, and then the original postman comes back in, and the other one becomes postman, and calls someone else outside. (I told you we were sophisticated!) On this occasion my beautiful friend Peg called Scottie out, and then, to my surprise, Scottie called me out. And the end of this story is... we never went back in!

What Scottie and I liked was hiking. We'd set off on a Sunday morning, maybe half past nine or ten o'clock. Sunday was our only day. Jimmy was in the band, and I worked at the Co-op all week, and rehearsed in my lunch hour for the rep., which I did every evening, for a pound a week. It was a good job I never had any parts that mattered. I was usually the maid bringing on a tray of coffee.

So our pleasure was hiking on a Sunday. Tomato and egg sandwiches and a thermos flask in a knapsack. We'd do twenty-five miles. If you walked along the Promenade to Hess Bank, then to Wharton Crag, Yealand Conyers or Yealand

Redmayne, that was a good long walk. Or we'd take the bus to Galgate and then walk back. If we were coming back by Arnside and Silverdale, on the side of a river there was a pub where you could get a 'whisky all in' for tenpence – 'whisky all in' was whisky with a piece of lemon and water. We'd have a tenpenny whisky and get a bus back home. We walked all over the place. It was lovely. Hiking – never hitch-hiking – was a main pastime in those days.

I'm happy when I'm hiking
Off the beaten track
Out in the open spaces,
La, la, *there and back,*
I'm la de da de de da
Knapsack on my back
With a real good friend, onto journey's end
Ten, twenty, thirty, forty, fifty miles a day.

(Well, it was a long time ago!)

DANCING

PRIVATE INSTRUCTION
Daily, 10 a.m. to 10 p.m.
(No appointment necessary)

TEA DANCES Daily
(including Sundays) 4-6.30.

The
Brayton Dance Club
Meeting every afternoon and evening
(including Sundays)

Quarterly Subscription - 10/6

Send for particulars to:–
THE BRAYTON GALLERIES,
316 Regent Street, W. 1
Phone: Mayfair 951.l

Chapter Ten

Transport and Communications

Nobody in Cheapside had a car. You hardly ever saw a car when I was a child, and we certainly didn't have one. Nevertheless, almost my very first words to Scottie, on the occasion of our meeting, when he had offered to walk my friend and me home from a dance, were, 'We have a car.'

We have a car! It was a boy called Edwin Sybil's Austin 7, about as big as a chocolate box, that used to get seven of us squeezed in for going to dances, and Edwin and his friend, Tolo Bullock, would usually run us home at the end. My best friend Peg and I had been to a late dance one Wednesday in the Winter Gardens ballroom, a shilling to go. Towards the end of this particular Wednesday night dance, Peg and I were both standing watching the dancing when two

gentlemen from the Winter Garden Variety
Orchestra came in and stood near us, and I found
I was standing next to Scottie... I can see him now,
in a black evening overcoat, with a long, white
evening scarf, one fringe end very near his chin,
the other end nearly on the floor, and a black,
snap-brimmed trilby. I thought, 'What a leading
man!' They started to chat to us, and they offered
to see us home, but with such pride I said, 'We
have a car!'

Although, as it happened, we didn't have a car.
When Peg and I left the Winter Gardens we were
just in time to see the Austin 7 go whizzing past...
they had left us behind! We started to walk home,
and we hadn't gone far before our two new
admirers, Scottie and Bill Glover, overtook us and
said, 'Have you been stood up?' How humiliating!
And that's how it all started between Scottie and
me, although, as I've told you, we didn't actually
'click' until our next meeting, at a party at
Dorothy Spencer's on 14 December, which was
two or three months later.

As I've mentioned, the heaviest traffic you were
ever likely to see down Cheapside in my childhood

were the horse-drawn trams of the Lancaster and District Tramways Company, which stopped outside the Royalty Theatre, and ran until 1921. The very last horse tramway in England was the Morecambe Tramways Company, which went from Strawberry Gardens to Bare, until it too closed in 1926. The Morecambe and Heysham Corporation introduced Morecambe and Heysham Tramway tickets from 1929, but they were actually for buses. We never had an electric tramway. We went straight from horses to buses, and increasingly, as the years went by, to private cars.

Although I'm no expert, I do remember some things about travelling in cars in the old days – things like crash gear boxes, where you had to change gear without benefit of a clutch and made an awful crunching sound if you didn't get it just right; cars with starting handles at the front that you had to turn to get the engine turning – and they usually *wouldn't* start until the man had nearly done himself an injury. It was always the men who drove, wearing leather driving gloves.

You signalled with elaborate hand signals – this is where women passengers sometimes joined in! You made a rather graceful circling motion to indicate you wanted to turn left. Later, cars got 'trafficators', a little handle with an orange light in the middle that popped up on either side of the car to indicate which way you were about to turn.

AA men rode about on motorbikes wearing gauntlets, leather helmets and goggles, and if you had an AA badge on the front of your car, they would give you a wave and a salute. I do rather miss those.

The dickey was the little seat at the back of a two-seater sports car – very cold and not at all comfortable! You needed your tartan travelling rug wrapped well round your knees if you were the gooseberry who had to ride on one of them.

Trains were all steam, and all the best stations had a railway hotel. The Midland Hotel at Morecambe was opposite the Midland Railway. Now we've still got the Midland Hotel, but the old station has moved. People took a lot of pride in the upkeep of their stations. They would have beautiful tubs of flowers along the platform, which was kept swept and clean, and a little vase of flowers on the table of the Ladies' Waiting Room. There would be a uniformed station master, who wore a top hat in the most important stations; several porters with hand-carts to help you with your luggage; a wheel tapper, who tapped the wheels with a little hammer – don't ask me what for; and of course the guard, with a flag and a whistle, who would call out, 'All aboard!' and wave his flag and blow his whistle to tell the driver to steam up again.

Nearly all the carriages were made up of a long corridor running down the side of the coach, and off it were the individual carriages, where six people could sit, three a side, with a net luggage rack over each banquette. There was often a mirror on one side, and a map of the train's route, with a photograph of Blackpool, or Margate, or whichever famous holiday resort the railway could take you to, on the other. The window was heavy, and had big leather loop handles for raising or lowering – 'Would you be so kind as to open the window for me?' a lady might ask a gentleman sitting in the same carriage

– and above the window was the Emergency Stop
Cord, that you pulled to stop the train at the risk
of incurring an enormous five pound fine for
'improper use'! I think it's a hundred pounds or
more today, isn't it? And there was always a
guard's van, where you could leave your big
luggage, like a trunk, or a dog or cat in a basket,
or bicycles, or any heavy stuff you didn't want
with you in your carriage, and the guard would
keep an eye on it. There was always the faint smell
of burning oranges.

Journeys took much longer, with the trains
stopping at many more stations and halts, with all
the level crossings operated by hand by the man
in the signal box, and places where the trains
would take on more water to help keep a head of
steam in the boiler. There were even some little
halts in the country where you stood on the
platform, held your hand up and the train
chuffed in and stopped, just for you. Early
morning local trains would even deliver
newspapers round the neighbourhood by
throwing them into your garden as they passed.
Overnight express trains would stop in the early

morning at tiny wayside stations and halts called things like Drem Junction, if passengers 'gave due notice to the guard' (and no doubt a silver coin or two changed hands).

Important or urgent news came by telegram. To send a telegram you would go into a post office and fill out a form – using as few words as possible to make sense of your message, because they charged you by the word. The message was printed out and sent down the wire to the nearest post office to the person you were sending it to, and delivered to them usually by a uniformed telegram boy. Living through two world wars, we were never very happy to see a telegram boy arriving at the door. There was always the worry about opening a telegram, in case it was dreadful news.

As time went by, you could send a telegram by speaking to the telephone operator. Spike Milligan, working on scripts on the top floor of his home, would pick up the telephone to send a telegram to his wife who was downstairs in the same house. There would be a knock on the door, and when she went to answer it there would be a telegram boy with a message which read things like, 'WHAT TIMES LUNCH STOP SPIKE.'

The other kind of telegram which wasn't too worrying for anybody was the wedding telegram – when friends who couldn't come to the wedding would traditionally send a supposedly amusing but usually, to at least half the guests, unintelligible and often extremely rude message of congratulation to the happy couple. The job of the hapless best man was to read them all out, but fortunately, by the time he did, the bride and groom and their guests were usually too far gone to even know who they were from.

When you did make a telephone call, you had to go through the local operator, and weren't they notorious for listening in to get all the gossip! If you wanted to call someone far away, you had to make a 'toll call', or a 'trunk call', and sometimes had to wait for the operator to call you back after she had gone through lots of other telephone exchanges to make the connection – all this is done in seconds by computers now, but in those days it all had to be done by professional telephone girls, in front of a switch-board with all those coloured plugs. These days you can speak to someone in Australia or America and they sound as if they are in the next room. In those days someone ten miles away sounded more as if they were a thousand miles away. 'Your time's up, caller,' the operator used to say, interrupting politely but firmly, so it was a quick dash to, 'Goodbye, goodbye!'

Then there were the public telephone boxes, with Buttons A and B, where to make a call you had to put your money in first, and when the person answered you had to press Button A, and the machine took your money. If they didn't answer, you pressed Button B and got your money back. It was a fixed amount for a local call, which changed from year to year. If you were making a long distance call from a telephone box, a trunk call, you had to dial 0 for the Operator first, and they would tell you how much money to put in, so you had to balance piles of different coins, shillings, sixpences and coppers, ready on the side. When she had connected you, she would say, 'Press Button A, please' and you would hear your money crashing through, or, if they couldn't connect you, they would say, 'Press Button B' so you could get your money back. After three minutes there would be pips, or, 'Your time's up, caller' and you'd have to put more money in, or you'd be cut off.

Very few people had their own telephone in their home. Some shops and post offices, and of course big businesses had to have them, but not many ordinary people. There might be one telephone in a neighbourhood. We didn't have one, ever, even after I was married, until we set up home in London after the war. My mother didn't ever have a telephone, so I have never in reality used one of those very early candlestick telephones, like the one they gave me for *In Loving Memory*, holding the earpiece against my earphone plaits and speaking down the handset in a posh voice, glancing in the mirror at my appearance – as if they could see me! I got that from my Auntie Nellie.

I was only five, and staying in Manchester with Auntie Nellie, who had a shop. I was having watercress for my tea, and my Auntie Nellie said,

'Now you eat up that watercress, because it's full of iron.' I thought, 'Oh! I don't want to eat any iron!' Just then the shop bell went, and she walked through the curtain to the shop and I heard her saying, 'Hello, Mrs Armitage!' in a very posh, refined sort of voice. Not like my Auntie Nellie's voice at all. When she came back, she spoke to me like her normal self again. I thought something funny just happened to her voice when she walked into the shop. It was a long time before it dawned on me that she deliberately put it on.

BLACKPOOL
The perfect springtime tonic

Blackpool's tonic sea air, its invigorating atmosphere, its lavish entertainment drive away the effects of Winter and give you the urge to do things.

Blackpool will help you to recover speedily that vital springtime fitness.

So come along to Blackpool and let Blackpool do you good.

A postcard to H. W. Foster, Town Hall, Blackpool, will bring Spring Folder and accommodation list post free.

Travel by L M S

... Third Class Monthly Return Tickets are only 1d. a mile (1½ a mile first class), and there are luxurious L M S trains to take you.

for healthy, happy holidays

Chapter Eleven
The Correct Dress

My father always wore fawn spats, with pearl buttons. Men wore them for warmth really, but they were also worn for a bit of 'dress up', and they were a fashion item. A prosperous business man would wear them. Spats are two pieces of felt or such-like material, that go over each instep, with a strap going underneath the sole of your shoes and buckled at the side. My father also had buttoned boots, of kid, with patent leather round the bottom. There was nothing 'pansy' about that – a well-dressed man wore those sort of things.

My father was a man who always dressed himself correctly. When he was the manager at the Royalty Theatre he wore dress clothes every night. He would greet the audience as they arrived to see the play, 'Good evening.' He knew all the people

who had regular seats. He would accompany
them to their seats, if they were in the dress
circle. Only the Queen gets that sort of treatment
these days.

You see good looking men nowadays, smart
men, leading men, wearing bow-ties, and what do
you see at the side? A buckle, because the bow-tie
is ready-tied and on a bit of elastic, and the game
is given away because their shirt collar won't sit
down flat. The reason that the shirt collar won't
keep down properly is that they no longer have
stud-holes. Shirt studs made the collar sit better,
flatter. You pushed them through the hole in the
shirt neck band, with the round bit of the stud
next to the neck, through the bit in the collar, and
it anchored everything. I've pictures of Jimmy
wearing his bow-tie, hand tied, neatly anchored.
Nobody does it right nowadays. You see them
riding up all over the place.

At Mrs Blundell's

For women and girls in my young day, life was
much more complicated than for boys and men.
We had all sorts of garments nobody wears

nowadays, and I sold dozens of them when I was a teenage shop assistant at Blundell's.

There was the modesty vest – the name describes it – to hide your cleavage. It would be a piece of material about eight or nine inches by ten, it could be in crepe de chine with a little bit of pretty lace at the top, or it could be in plain white lawn, with a bit of embroidery at the top. You pinned it in with little gilt safety pins on any dress, a cross-over dress for instance, that showed your cleavage. I never actually wore one myself, but I've sold many a dozen, when I was working at Blundell's. (In the evening you showed your cleavage – and you would have a bare back. That was considered all right.) The plain white ones started at elevenpence halfpenny, and there was a rare assortment, the ultimate being crepe de chine and lace – for three and elevenpence three farthings (or we would say, 'three and eleven, three') – just like the nine pounds 99p you get charged these days.

A liberty bodice was a little jacket without sleeves, and it would have tapes stitched on with suspender buttons, to keep your stockings up.

(I never wore stockings, though. I wore socks all the time I was at school.) They were for children. I always wore one in the winter, with a fleecy lining. Not a sheep fleece, but material that was a bit fleecy. You wore your bodice over your vest. There were no whalebones in them, so they were more comfortable than a corset. They cost one and elevenpence halfpenny, and buttoned down the front, with bone buttons.

Combinations were very popular. Combinations (or combs for short) were like a bathing suit, and they buttoned all up the front. They had long sleeves, and sometimes the legs came right down to your knees. At the back was a piece of material that went between your legs, with a flap that tucked in, so you could go to the loo without stripping right down. They were warm for the winter – because it was so cold in the north before the days of central heating. They were quite expensive in pure wool, or less dear, in cotton. Your combs would go on first, and they did for a vest as well. You didn't wear a bra with them, because they were made with inlets which gave you support. Then you wore your corsets over the top.

We had men's combs as well – a vest and pants all in one. Longjohns were trouser-length underpants for men. There were men's tie-pins, those smooth ones, on a 'spiffy' box outside Blundell's, a box of stylish things like hat pins, safety pins, tie-pins … and everything was a penny each.

We even sold shrouds, at Blundell's, for people who didn't want to go to an undertaker, and were laying out at home. But I never sold one.

Camisoles were very fashionable – you still get those today – little tops with lace straps, for under a blouse. Silk. Crepe de chine. Fine lawn. They were very pretty. Little bits of ribbon threaded through. Little bows on. You could have a vest on, too, perhaps, underneath, but the camisole would hide it. I've two camisoles at home.

Bloomers – now they were very unbecoming. Long pants with big wide legs. Only women who lived alone, or who didn't care what their husbands thought of their appearance, wore those.

Until I was about ten I always wore little knickers, with an insertion in the legs for pink or blue ribbon with a bow at the side, with little frilled edges. And vests that came down over your bottom, with little sleeves, not a strap. And in the winter at school you had thick navy blue knickers with a pocket in them, that you wore under a gym slip.

Sunday best

You always had new 'best' clothes bought for you at Whitsuntide. You might get a new two-piece suit, or costume as we called it, and shoes, or a new coat and dress. So then your Sunday best clothes, that you'd had for the year before, became your Saturday clothes. You wore a gymslip to school all week, but on Saturday you wore your mufti, your Saturday clothes. You used to talk about it, 'What are you having for Whitsun?'

Chapter Twelve
That Ol' Time Religion

I think I was about five, and Neville was about six and a half, when we started going to Sunday School.

Miss Hindle, our Sunday School teacher, was very good at telling stories. I loved that. She was from a Lancashire mill town, so she didn't speak with a Morecambe dialect. She would say, 'Them there shepherds saw yon angel...' It made it all sound more exciting, somehow. I remember once being invited to tea at her house at Wellington Terrace. She had a hat on. Who would sit at tea wearing a hat in their own home these days? Even if they were entertaining a six year old visitor!

We had a Sunday School bazaar one year. The girls were taught how to make little lavender bags, three inches by two of muslin, with a ribbon drawn through, stuffed with dried lavender, which you put in amongst your handkerchiefs, or your mother would put them between pillowcases in a drawer. Then Miss Hindle had the bright idea of putting the lads on knitting dishcloths. They were each given a big ball of the thick stringy stuff dishcloths are made from. She put fifty stitches on wooden knitting needles, and showed the boys how to do the knitting. When my brother had done three inches, he'd somehow got seventy stitches on his needles. A bit further on there were thirty. You've never seen anything like the shapes of these dishcloths. Miss Hindle had to pull them all back, unravel them, and say, 'Thank you lads. You can finish these next week.' But of course none of these dishcloths were ever finished or sold. They were all full of runs and dropped stitches and extra stitches.

We made friends there which lasted right through to Chapel days, friends that we only met on a Sunday, because they didn't live near Cheapside. When you were old enough to go to Chapel on a Sunday night, it wasn't that you were old enough to go, it was that you were old enough to come home at night without your mother and father having to come and collect you. But I'm afraid we often only went because there was nothing else to do. The backs of the hymn books were plain paper, and we all sat together in two pews and played noughts and crosses. Isn't it awful? It wasn't that we didn't believe in God, but you did have to spend a lot of time in chapel in those days, and a lot of it was boring for young people.

When the Queen's Cinema started showing films on a Sunday night – I was in my teens before that happened – most of us would go there after chapel. Sodom and Gomorrah wasn't in it! You'd hear people talking about it, 'What about the Queen's Cinema then? Disgraceful! You'd think they'd have something better to do on a Sunday night!' I'm afraid there was a lot of hypocrisy about church-going in those days. My friend Margaret Willacy, from one of the great Morecambe fishing families, wasn't allowed to go to the cinema on a Sunday. Her father later became Mayor of Morecambe.

One of the people who impressed Scottie and me
most, when we had moved to London just after
the war, was a parson at St Dunstan's – Bill Spate
– who had himself been blinded in the '14–18 war,
on the day he was twenty-one. He was a great
man. He never seemed blind because he had
learned so many ways of adapting. He had
counted the number of steps he took from his gate
to his front door, from his gate to each of the
shops, so he walked along quite quickly, and you
wouldn't know he couldn't see. When we took
him out to dinner at Simpson's it was interesting
because he would say, 'Put the salt at three o'clock,
please.' Or, 'Put the mustard at nine o'clock.' And
then he knew exactly where they were.

Once we were taking him to St Dunstan's in
Princess Crescent, in Regent's Park, near the zoo,
where he was preaching. It was very foggy, a real
pea-souper. Jimmy was driving, but at an absolute
crawl, and I said, 'I hate this fog, when you can't
see, don't you, Bill?' And he said, 'Well... um. I
would, wouldn't I?'

I said, 'Why would you... ? Aaaaaagh!' I never
remembered with Bill.

He once told me a story that he said was true,
about a church in America where an old black
man had always gone from when he was a boy,
when it had started as just a room in a poor part
of town. It had grown into a large church and
more and more well-to-do people moved into the
area and went there. A group of women who
belonged to the church, who did a lot to raise
money for the church, began objecting to him
being there, because he was the only coloured
man. They said to the minister, 'He doesn't live
round here. Can't you tell him to go to his own
local church?' The minister said, 'But he's been
coming here since he was a little boy. What am I
going to say to him?'

'Oh, you'll think of something.'

So the minister says to this old black man,
'There's a church near to where you live, isn't there?'

And the man said, 'Yes, there is.'

'So why don't you go to that?'

'Because I come here. I've come here since I
was a little boy.'

And the minister said, 'Well, I wouldn't hurt
you for the world, but you know some of the

women who donate most of the money which keeps this church going, object to your being here because you're black. So do you think you could go to your own church?'

And the man is broken-hearted, but he says, 'I will. But why? Why don't they want me?'

The minister said, 'I don't know what to say to you, Joseph. Ask God – perhaps he can tell you the answer.'

He didn't see him again for two years, and then one day he saw him out on the street, so he went across to him and said, 'Hallo, Joseph. How are you?'

And Joseph said, 'Hallo, minister. I'm fine.'

'Did you find another church to go to?'

'Yes. I did.'

'And did you ask God why we asked you to leave the church?'

'I did.'

'Can I ask you what God said?'

'You can. He said, "Joseph, I've been trying to get into that church myself for years... and never managed it!"'

FREE CHURCH TOURING GUILD

£39 17 6	GRAND ITALIAN TOUR via St. Gothard and Simplon. Short Sea Route
£16 16	VENICE, STRESA (for Lake Maggiore) GARDONE-RIVIERA (for Lake Garda)
£12 12	LUGANO, 14 Days, Excursions, MILAN LAKE COMO (Menaggio, Bellagio)
£10 10	LAKE OF LUCERNE, 14 days' Hotels, Extensions Grindelwald, Engelberg etc.
£5 5	BRUGES, YPRES, ZEEBRUGGE including journey and 7 days' Hotels, with 3 Excursions.
£7 7	BELGIAN SEA-COAST HOLIDAY including journey and 14 days' Hotels, with 3 Excursions.

Secretary, 113, Memorial Hall,
Farringdon Street, E. C. 4

Chapter Thirteen
The Co-op Divi

It was called the Fielden Wood System. Everyone who was a Co-op member had a gummed sheet about three and a half inches wide and about ten inches long. The assistants tore off a 'check', as they called them, like a receipt, with the amount you had spent written on it, and it was given to you with your change. Those checks were stuck on your gumsheet, and when the gumsheet was full you took it to the Co-op office in Northumberland Street, where they gave you an orange total sticker, on top of your next gumsheet, and at the end of each quarter you got two shillings in the pound and a twopenny bonus. That's what I bought Jan's first pram with, my Co-op divi.

A couple who owned the chemist near the Co-op, where I worked, had had a Rolls-Royce pram for their baby, and once the baby was out of the big pram they wanted to sell it (the pram, not the baby). I was in there one day and remarked on how beautiful it was. They said, 'Well, if you know anybody who's expecting, we're selling it.' I was about two months pregnant at the time, and nobody knew but Jimmy and me. So with my Co-op dividends together with some silver threepenny bits I had saved, I bought that pram for Jan.

In my job as cashier at the Co-op, in the days of old money, I used to have eight shillings laid out in squares – four two-shilling pieces, then a row of shillings, then a row of pennies in piles of five. So if someone sent a ten-bob note up, and they'd spent two and sevenpence, I'd go, 'Sevenpence... a shilling, two shillings, ten bob.' Bong, you had your change. Three movements did it. Everyone had their own system that worked for them, and that was mine.

The assistants would always say to the customers, 'Will that be all? No tea? Coffee? Right. One and nine, one and nine, one and nine, two

and three, two and three, two and three, three and
eleven, three and eleven, five and ten, five and
ten...' and add it up like that, and then tell them
what it was. I would take the money and check
out of the cup that had whizzed up along the
overhead wire, and put the check back on the
cup, and then put the change on top, which
weighed it down, and then I whizzed it back
to the counter. I had a girl with me, doing the
booking, so I'd say, 'One and nine – grocery' as
I put the change in, and she wrote it down in a
book, and that was your summary. When the
shop closed you compared your summary with
your takings, to get them right, to see they
all tallied.

Mrs Newton, who was on the Committee, said,
'That was a pound note I just gave you.' It was
a brown pound note in those days, and a red
ten-shilling note. There was a red ten-shilling
note sitting on the top of the cup. I said, 'No.
I'm sorry. It's a ten-shilling note.' She said, 'I'll
get you the sack for this!' and George Ormrod,
on Provisions, said, 'It was a ten-shilling
note, Mrs.'

'It was a *pound* note. I'm on the Committee. I'm not going to try and do a store for ten shillings, am I?'

So I gave her change for a pound, and later I said to my mother 'Would you mind doing without a check on your order?' She said, 'Yes, all right.' Which meant my mother went without her divi, but it straightened my money up. After that I said to George Ormrod, 'From now on, if you send a ten-shilling note up, on the right hand side of the check put a half. If it's a pound, put a one. Then we've no argument.' So we did that, it was my idea, and there was never any trouble after that.

Later, when I was working at the Emporium at Regent Road, it was still the Co-op, but much bigger. They had furniture and carpets and men's outfitting. But there was still only one cashier – me. All the stations had D numbers, from one to ten. (It was complicated – but when you're young your mind can do these things very quickly. Like kids with computers today.) I had two girls booking for me there. That was a pneumatic suction system, with a little cup that the assistant

opened, the money was put in, and it flopped
down into a trough and was sent whizzing along
the overhead tube to the office where I was, by
pneumatic suction. The engine was working all
the time, so the whole room I was in shuddered,
and I thought of all this money, coming towards
me from every direction. I would open the little
cup, take the money out, lay the little slip with the
amount on top of the cup and say to the booker,
'Twopence halfpenny, haberdashery, D4.' I'd put
the right change on top of the slip, close the cup,
and send it back by pulling a wooden handle. The
cup went whizzing back along the tube and
flopped back into the net at the counter where the
customer was, and the assistant there gave them
their change. I had my change ready, and at the
Emporium, by heck we were busy on a Saturday,
or on the first day of the sale... two thousand
pounds they took, in one day. I loved it when it
was busy. I loved the competition of it, but I did
nearly have a nervous breakdown when I was
working there.

I had a buttoned overall, with sleeves, white cuffs.
I learned all sorts of things. At Queen's Road I
learned how to cut half a pound of lard dead
on. Lard came in boxes. George Ormrod, at the
provisions counter, with the bacon, cheese and
lard for sale, would get a box of lard and he could
cut a 28-pound box of lard into 56 half-pound
pieces, exactly. The greaseproof paper was in a
pile, and as he cut the lard he kept the knife in it
and lifted the paper by the lard sticking on it. He
was like a machine, he could do it so fast. I said to
him, 'You're making me dizzy.' He said, 'Come
and try it.' One afternoon when we were quiet I
managed to cut up 56 perfect half-pounds of lard.
He said, 'Right. You've got that now. Perfect. And
you'll never do it again.' He was quite right. I
never did!

The butter came in a barrel. The different
rolls of bacon were on three marble steps. The
customer would say, 'I'll have half a pound of
Greenback, please, George. Cut it at seven.' On the
bacon slicer they could set it to a numbered scale,
from very thin to thick, so the customers got to
know what the number of the thickness was that

they liked. In its old fashioned way, it was quite a sophisticated system. If a woman came in who you knew had a big family, you'd know she would want it sliced very thin. They would get flitch bacon, which is fatty, what we call streaky today, and they might ask him to cut it at thirteen – which is nearly tissue paper thin.

It was all very hierarchical, in those days. The boss was the manager, Mr Rose, who was rather quiet, but not the easiest of men; then later on it was Mr Simpson, who we all liked. Under him, Bert Davis was first hand, like first mate on a ship. Bert Davis was six foot three. He could bend over the counter and pick up a box off the shop floor, and he could see everything that went on over the far side of the counter. George Ormrod would be next to Bert in seniority. Then there was Billy Earnshaw, who had a set of false teeth, every other one gold, but he only wore them on a Saturday. We had this long ladder, steps we called them, for the top shelves, which were packed with tinned fruit. Every Saturday morning, when the whole shop was full, Billy would be at the top of these steps, stacking the shelves, singing a very long song called *The Farmer's Boy* all about a boy who gets a job working on a farm for a kind hearted couple, and ends up marrying the daughter and inheriting the farm. '*The farmer's wife said, "Try the lad..."*' On and on he'd go, through all the verses, '*The farmer's boy grew up a man...*'

And we'd be saying, 'Are you coming down to help serve, Billy?'

'In a minute. *...and the good old couple died...*'

And the women would shout, 'We know, Billy, we know he gets the farm and he gets the girl – you sing it every blooming Saturday. Now will you come and serve!'

The only female assistant was Edith Mayer. She was a distant cousin of my mother's. She was four foot nine wet through, must have been sixty, and had worked at the Co-op for ever. She had to stand on a little square wooden box to put the cup in, with the money, and she was rather short-sighted. The remarks the men used to make about her!

We only had one lavatory for all the staff, men and women – which wouldn't be allowed these days. It was through in the back shop. We always knew when Miss Mayer was going, because she used to hum a little tune under her breath, as she passed me at my cash desk, and George Ormrod at Provisions, 'Dum, de, dum, te, tiddly tum, di ti, ti di...' We had a wax model of a boy, to dress the window, in a spotless white apron and coat, holding out a basket of goods. One day Billy Earnshaw put this model boy inside the loo. We all heard her, 'Dum, de, dum, te, tiddly tu–' Then as she opened the door, 'Oh, sorry...' and off she went back to her place. After she'd gone through to the back for the eighth time... 'Dum, de, dum, te, tiddly tum, di ti... Oh, sorry...' I was afraid she was going to burst. They were like that though – wicked.

Jimmy – I've forgotten his surname – had had his own little grocer's shop, but it went bust and so he had a job at the Co-op. Now, in the summer, with all the visitors, you sold them what they asked for and got on to serve the next one quick. But not Jimmy – how silly that I've forgotten what his second name was, he was such a dear man. The customer would say, 'Quarter of tea, please.' And Jimmy would say, 'Threepence halfpenny,

fourpence halfpenny... or sixpenny – very suitable
to the waters of the district?' (I liked that touch –
'tea that is suitable to the waters of the district!')
The others would say to him, 'Don't go through
all the different teas, Jimmy, just give 'em the
eightpenny one.' But Jimmy was serving them in
the same courteous way that he had in his own
little shop.

Women customers had their own favourite
assistants, 'I'll wait for you, Roly.' That was Roly
Spate, who looked like Edward G. Robinson. 'All
right, Mrs Jackson.' And Roly would know what
she wanted. He lived at Heysham. He took me to
the pictures once, the Queen's, one Sunday night,
with a cap on, and spats. He looked so attractive.

We had an assistant there, Tom Tyson, seventy-
two, who should have finished years ago, but he
wouldn't be sacked. At every meeting they would
say, 'We've got to sack Tyson.' But he always said,
'I don't want to be sacked. I don't want to be stuck
at home.' So he stayed on. His apron was so long it
touched his insteps. Holiday visitors in those days
took rooms, but bought their own food and gave
it to the landlady to prepare or cook for them.

A woman came in one Monday, and there was one two-pound loaf left from the Saturday, but the fresh ones hadn't come in yet. She said, 'A large loaf, please.' Tom brought this stale loaf over and banged it down in front of her. Not a crumb fell off, it was that hard. She said, 'Oh! No, a fresh one, please.'

They were fourpence halfpenny, a two-pound loaf in those days – think of the difference now! Tom looked hard at her for a few seconds and then said, 'Fourpence.'

'No, no,' she said. 'No, it's a fresh one I'd like.'

He pushed it an inch towards her. 'Threepence halfpenny.'

'No! You don't seem to understand. It isn't the price I'm worried about – it's the loaf. I want a fresh one.'

'Threepence.'

'*No.*'

Finally, he pushes it at her and says, 'D' you keep 'ens?'

Your order would be sent round in a good wooden box, a beautiful box that perhaps the tinned salmon had been delivered to the shop in.

George West drove the van.

Another assistant was Sammy, with bright red hair, and last but not least, Willy Wilson, the junior assistant, whose father was a captain in the Salvation Army. Willy was a little lad who was longing to wear a long white apron like the other assistants, but the others said he had to 'earn his uniform'. They used to tease him unmercifully. They would send him off to get ridiculous things like, 'Go to Edgar Bell's and ask for a small tin of Frogs' Knee Paste. A small one mind. Now what have you to get?'

'A small tin of Frogs' Knee Paste.' And off he'd trot – he never seemed to see through them. When he came back empty handed they'd shake their heads as if they were very disappointed in him.

If the assistants were all 'characters', so were many of our customers.

Mrs Bradley walked up and down outside the shop on a Saturday night. Timing? She should have been an actress. There were two narrow doors into the shop, which rang a bell when you

opened them. She walked up and down outside
from twenty-five past six – we closed at half past
six on a Saturday – and just as they were going to
close the doors, whisht! She was in. I used to
watch out for this, because it was so funny. She
was four foot nine, and she had about eight kids.
Mr Rose used to say to her, 'Why don't you come
in earlier?' But she was waiting, you see, because
she knew that things like pies, bread and cakes
couldn't be kept until the following Monday, so
she'd be given a lot of stuff very cheap, or even
free. And there was a Mrs Iredale, who had a lot of
hens and used to come in for two stones of split
corn and Indian meal. She was always sucking on
a bit of Indian meal. I've played her.

I learned so much about character acting from
watching them all, observing them – in real life
people are often much funnier than in any
comedy script. It was ten years of my life – and
it was well spent. I don't regret one minute of it.
Not one minute – of getting to know people. And
married to Scottie – that's another fifty-eight years
I wouldn't give a minute back. I've really had a
wonderful life.

Chapter Fourteen

My Mother,
God Bless Her

My grandad Hird, the skipper, was a sea-trader who did business on the high seas, and one day he went missing. He never came home. My father always used to say, 'If he walked in that door now, I would shoot him!' And Neville used to say, 'What with?'

'Never mind what with! What he did to my mother!'

Years later, his schooner was found in a cave in the Hawaiian islands, with the log book and everything, so they knew that the skeletons were my grandad and his crew. Mr Spencer, an old professor who had a good wall of shelves of books, lived in a street near us. He came round to our house one day, with a book with a piece of paper in, marking the place, and he said to my father,

'James, read this.' It was all about how this man had found a schooner, and the log book had written in it *James Hird – Captain and Owner.* That was the first time we knew what had happened to him.

My grandmother Hird, his wife, had died years before this, when I was about two. I can remember standing on a bentwood chair while my mother fastened two little pearl buttons on my pink crepe de chine dress, saying, 'Stand still.' A little mob cap I had on. My cousin Edna, our Nev and I had to stand at the other side of the hedge at the Todmorden Cemetery while the coffin was lowered into the grave, because they thought it might affect us to see it.

My grandparents Mayer, on my mother's side, I never knew at all. They were dead long before I was born. My grandmother was a Birkett, one of the daughters of Dalham Towers. Marriage to a Morecambe fisherman, who called ladies 'yadies', wasn't what they had intended for their daughter at all. We had silver napkin rings, from my grandmother Birkett, and pure white linen serviettes.

My favourite image of my mother, I can see her now, looking up over the paper, 'Oh, I see Lady Cynthia So-and-so's getting married...' she'd say to whoever was in the room. 'Of course her mother, you know, was the Duke of So-and-so's eldest daughter. Oh yes. There were three daughters, but her mother was the eldest. A wonderful family. Because *her* mother was...' And she'd start going even further back – she'd know the whole family tree of all the great families!

My mother was a true blue Conservative, through and through, and my brother was Labour – he was treasurer and secretary for the Morecambe and District Labour Party. It wasn't communist or anything like that. Ted Shore and the lads wouldn't hurt a fly. But my mother used to say, 'I cannot understand you, Neville!' As though he were a criminal or something. He'd say, 'No, well that's it, you see, Marie. You *don't* understand. Because if you *did* understand – you'd vote Labour!'

'Never! Never!' As though he'd called her a dirty name.

'No, well, it's Mr Singleton you're going to vote for?'

'Of course I am.'

'Do you know what he stands for?'

'He's a Conservative.'

'Apart from that, Marie?' And he'd go on teasing her until my father or I would say, 'Will you shut up – we keep hearing the same script.'

But she'd always stick up for him. When my father would say, looking up at the clock, and seeing it was ten past ten, 'Pubs have closed. Where is he?', she'd always say, 'No, well, Jim, he'll be round the lamp, talking politics.' Dad would go to the front door, and there they were round the street lamp, Neville and his cronies – about six or seven of them. They ran the country, round that lamp. But if it was me, still out at ten past ten – which I very rarely was, because we weren't goody-goodies, but if they said 'ten o'clock' that's when we were in – then it would be my mother who would say, 'Well where has she got to now?' And it would be my father who would say, 'Ah! Give her a minute, Polly!' It was so blatant in our house.

My brother smoked. And like any other young fellow, by Thursday night he hadn't any money left because he wasn't paid until Friday. My mother ruined my brother – well, if he'd been a lesser man, she would have. She used to buy ten Robin cigarettes, in a little yellow packet, with a picture of a robin. They were sixpence for ten. She 'secreted' this packet behind an ornament on the mantelpiece, but I don't know why she bothered, because we all knew it was there. On the Thursday night, Nev would always say, 'If I had a cigarette, I'd have one. But I haven't...' And then, after a bit, 'Now, Marie, you wouldn't have a cigarette, would you?' And you knew she was going to say, 'Well, just as it happens...' and produce the packet from behind the ornament. Every week it was the same script, the same performance. It was a ritual, and if it hadn't happened by Thursday tea-time, I'd be waiting for it. I'd be thinking, 'Go on. When are you going to say, "If I had a cigarette..." ' and he always did in the end.

I used to love watching my mother's face when she and Neville and I played whist. My mother would put cards down to help him win – and he was her opponent! I used to say to her, 'What are you doing?'

'What do you mean?'

'Well you know that card is going to get him that lot...'

'Yes. Well?'

'Well what are we playing cards for? Like silly devils?'

'No. Well...' But she adored him.

When she was bed-ridden, when I was in rep. at the Royalty, I used to nip down the back street to our back door, and in to her bedroom to ask her how I looked. She'd always tell me if I had too much make-up on, and soften any hard lines. Once I was playing an old charlady. At her suggestion I bought a stick of celery and left it out of water for two days, so the top flopped over, and I put it in the top of the shopping basket. You could hear people in the stalls tittering, 'Look at her celery!'

At the ambulance hall and places like that, there would often be a fancy dress dance. People used to come to my mother and say, 'Will you help me dress up as a gypsy, Mrs Hird?'

She'd say, 'Have you got any ear-rings?'

'No.'

'Have you any beads?' We kept a biscuit box full of beads and curtain rings for gypsy ear-rings, and she'd make them up.

I would wheel Jan in her Co-op divi pram to my mother's when I went along to the theatre. She would undress her and get her ready for bed, wash and iron the clothes she'd come in, and hold her in her arms, sitting in the little rocking chair that she sat in during the day.

Jan was just two when my mother died. My parents were staying with us over Christmas. My mother had been a sick woman, almost bed-ridden, for a long time. All my friends came in to see her and wish her a happy New Year. She died, still staying with us, at the end of January. I had put Jan's cot next to my mother's bed, and the next morning when I went in, she had died in her sleep, with her arm stretched out to the baby's cot.

If somebody died in Morecambe, on the day of the funeral everybody in their street would draw their curtains, or pull down their blinds, as a mark of respect. And often the next street as well – or along the route to the cemetery. It just depended on how well known they were, or how popular.

The day my mother was buried, I don't think there was a curtain left open in the town. She had helped everybody. She was a kind of stalwart. They'd come and tell her anything, to get it off their chest. My father used to look at her tired, kind face in the firelight, and say, 'You'll kill yourself with kindness to other people.' And she used to smile and say, 'Well it won't be a bad way to go.'

My father stayed on in the house after my mother died. He would come and visit Scottie and me in London quite often, to see me in things as my acting career began to take off, and he, too, died in my home, our London home. But his own home remained Cheapside, Morecambe, next to the Royalty Theatre where he had once been manager. He never wanted for people to look in and make sure he was all right, to bring him home-made meals, and to do anything at all for him. Nothing was too much trouble. Much as I've written about Cheapside – all the generosity of my mother came back to them in the end.

Chapter Fifteen

'The Duration'

I was sitting next to the Duke of Norfolk (ahem!) quite recently, at a charity luncheon at the Hilton. His wife was sitting opposite him. He was telling me about his life and saying, 'Of course I'm very old. I was born during the '14–18 war...'

'Oh well!' I said, 'That's nothing. I did my first concert during the First World War. I can remember quite clearly, I sang *When grandmama was quite a little girl*. It was for the wounded soldiers and they...'

I thought he was going to jump out of his seat. His face lit up.

'Oh!' he said, 'I haven't heard anybody say "wounded soldiers" for... well, I don't know how long!'

'Darling!' he said to his wife, 'Dame Thora here

– this wonderful lady – is talking about "wounded soldiers" – *nobody* says that now, do they? Soldiers who have received wounds, victims of war... even "war wounded men" perhaps – but never "wounded soldiers". Oh!' he said, turning back to me and seizing my hand, 'You are the nicest and most interesting Lancashire woman I have ever met... Yes you *are*!'

(As though I'd said, 'No, I'm not' – which I hadn't.)

I said, 'Yes, and they all wore bright blue suits, in thick flannel, and a bright red plain tie. I can see them now, sitting in rows in the Albert Hall, Morecambe, some with their heads swathed in bandages, some with a leg off...'

I remember that concert so well, at the Albert Hall at Morecambe. I wore a paisley shawl that had to be folded into eight, because I was so small. It was so heavy, I was crouching under it. I was four. And I wore a bonnet and sang,

When grandmama was quite a little girl
She dressed just in this style.
And I

> *Shall try*
> *This costume for a while.*
> *Although you think*
> *That it is rather quaint*
> *And* something da de da-a-a...
> *I like the clothes they wore the best*
> *When grandmama was quite a little girl.*

I was given my own Red Cross nurse's uniform, pinned on a piece of cardboard. A whole outfit, for tenpence. There was a little apron with a bib, the bib turned under, there was the head thing, everything with a little red cross on it – and oh, I did want to be a nurse. I wanted the war to last long enough, so I could grow up and nurse the wounded soldiers.

The other thing I remember vividly about the wounded soldiers, are the men who sang in the street after the war – the wounded ex-servicemen, out of work, walking along the middle of the road, never on the pavement, singing for money, rather than just begging. We saw dozens of them over the years. Usually it would be just one man, in a shabby mac, often with an arm or a leg missing, trudging along, singing, and my mother would always say, 'Oh, God help him. Take him a penny.' She used to say it with such feeling, it always made me feel sad the way she'd say, 'Oh, God help him...'

I was in a play called *Future Outlook Unsettled* at the Empire in Nelson. When Neville Chamberlain told us we were at war with Germany, I was bathing Jan, who was a baby, on the kitchen table in my digs. My mother was with us, and all we wanted to do was to get home, in case the Germans invaded Morecambe.

I can remember on the journey home thinking, 'Now what can I do?' Scottie immediately decided to volunteer for the minesweepers – a lot of nonsense, I told him. I said, 'Why volunteer? You'll get called up anyway.' But he said, 'No. I'd like to volunteer. You know.' Then he volunteered for the RAF, and they took him.

I knew a warrant officer in Morecambe, and he said they'd be wanting people for the billeting office, at the Clarendon Hotel. So I went there to work.

I was still in the rep. at a pound a week. The bus came at 12.30 from the Battery pub, and it arrived outside the Clarendon Hotel about a minute later. I used to come outside at exactly half past twelve for my lunch hour, get on the bus, go down to Central, a two and a half minute twopenny bus-ride, and my mother, waiting at home next door to the theatre, would have made me some sandwiches. I would rehearse for three quarters of an hour, and get the bus back.

I had the desk in the window at the Clarendon, because being in the local rep., people knew me, and if there were any complaints the landlady would be told to talk to me, because they knew she'd finish up by saying, 'Saw you last week, Thora, in *Yellow Sands*.'

There were fourteen of us in the billeting office. Thirteen smoked – everyone except me. But they kept saying, 'Oh go on, Hirdie – try one.' And eventually I did start to smoke there. Ashton's cigarettes, in a tin. With an oblique pattern – half the tin was cream and half was red. Two bob for thirty.

Of course, I'd pretended to smoke, as a teenager, going to dances with my friend Peg. Craven 'A' ('For the throat' it said, and I'm sure it meant that they gave you a bad throat) were ten for sixpence, so it was threepence a week each, and we would have two each on a Wednesday night, three each on a Saturday – just to hold them. Ten to one if we ever took a puff we ended up choking. But there we'd be, between dances, with coffee or lemonade in one hand, sitting in the *fauteuils*, holding the fag between two stiff fingers... sophisticated or what?

Before I took up smoking myself, I persuaded my father to smoke Ardath cigarettes, because they gave coupons, and for five hundred coupons you could get a portable gramophone. I eventually got one, in a red case. He usually smoked Gold Flake, but he smoked Ardath to get me a manicure set – a little oval base, with a half hoop over it of tortoiseshell, with little hooks on, with a file, a cuticle pusher, a pair of scissors, and at the bottom a tiny bottle of polish, and one of remover – and then the gramophone. Then he said, 'No more. That's it.

We stop now please. You're killing me.' He didn't like Ardath.

We were billeting soldiers and airmen with people in Morecambe. I quite enjoyed it. I'd done a night-school course in accountancy and book-keeping, so I felt I could do it. A landlady on Albert Road might have been posted with 'Twenty men, W/E breakfasts' (with effect breakfasts, or 'Wef' – which meant they would be in for breakfast). All that was entered down, and we paid her accordingly. A corporal went round every Friday, with an officer and a box of envelopes full of money to pay the landladies. The envelopes were left unsealed, and the landladies stood and counted it – 'Just a minute. I think you've given me one short, here, look, that should be one more Wef tea on the Wednesday...'

I went round with the officer myself once, because I asked to. In one house, there were notices on the walls: 'No leaning your rifles against this wallpaper.' 'Take your boots off before going upstairs.' I said to her, 'You've got two sons, haven't you, Mrs C–?'

'Yes.'

'And are they billeted somewhere?'

She said, 'Well, they were, but now they're away on active service.'

I said, 'And was there all this – no guns against the walls – take your boots off...?'

She said, 'Well, I don't know.'

I said, 'You'd have played merry hell if there had been, wouldn't you? These boys are doing their bit for their country. It doesn't mean, because they're in uniform, they're all badly behaved.'

She saw my point, I'm glad to say.

A lot took their stair-carpets up completely. Just bare boards. I said to one landlady, 'This will be nice and noisy, won't it?'

'Ah well, I'd only just had it laid. I don't want all those dirty boots going up and down.'

I said, 'Well couldn't you have covered it with a drugget (floor covering) or something? Whatever must this sound like?'

I don't suppose the men minded, but I thought that as the women were being paid for looking after them, at least they should be made to feel welcome. The officer said to me afterwards, 'I'd never thought of saying things like that.'

I said, 'Well, I'm probably saying it because my husband is an airman, and I know he's billeted somewhere – some of these women are treating them as though they were animals.'

And the complaints, nearly every Monday! Some woman might come and say, 'Now look, I had eleven in – see there it says, "Wef teas". They come in. They've had their teas – and then they had their supper... you see?'

And I'd say, 'And what are we being shown this for?'

'Well, 'cos you've only paid me for Wef teas – and it should have been Wef suppers – you see?'

So I'd say, 'Oh yes? And what did they have – a dry biscuit or something?' I could get them laughing, sometimes. It was up to me whether we paid them or not, so I was the one they were rather nice to. Sergeant Scott said to me, 'You're very patient with them.' I said, 'Well I've got to be, otherwise they'll take it out on the lads.'

In the RAF Jimmy was being moved from one place to another, and the next thing we knew, he was being sent to the RAF base at Morecambe. I saw the coming-in sheet, and I saw 1221348 Scott, J. LAC (Leading Aircraftsman) on the list. I went to our Sergeant in Charge – also called Scott, funnily enough, a really nice fellow – and I said, 'Do you know what I was thinking, sergeant?'

He said, 'No. What?'

I said, 'I was thinking, what with that house I've got, just for me and a small baby, I ought really to be billeting an airman... doing my bit for the war.'

He said, 'I've seen this list as well as you, you know. So I don't know what you're doing all this acting for. I'm not daft. 1221348, Scott, J., that's your husband, isn't it? Well, all right, he's boarded on you.'

So he was. He was billeted with me at Prompt Corner for the next six months. We didn't see a lot of him, even then. When he was on night duty, he'd set off on the push-bike, and come home and sleep during the day. Once I was travelling on a train with Jan, who was just a little girl, and an airman got in with us, and Jan said, 'Hallo, Daddy.'

I left the garden to Jimmy. He 'dug for victory' by planting a few rows of cabbages, when he was home, and soon after that he was sent away on active service.

I was in London for most of the war, living in digs in Perivale, and working at the Vaudeville Theatre in *No Medals*, with Fay Compton. Jan was looked after by her wonderful nanny, Vera. Every three weeks I would go home to see them, after the last show on Saturday night, on the five to eleven train from Euston to Lancaster. It took until six in the morning to get home to Morecambe. There were big notices at the stations, 'Is Your Journey Really Necessary?' to try and discourage people from travelling. 'Oh no,' I'd think, 'I'm just doing this for the fun of the thing.'

Billy Kiggings used to meet the papers off the train at Lancaster station, and I used to sit on a pile of newspapers in his van, from Lancaster to Morecambe, because he had to pass the top of our lane, and then I'd walk down. On Monday I'd have to catch the 6.45 a.m. boat train from the Midland Station back to Euston. It got into

London at 1 p.m. – and I'd do two shows that night.

I remember getting into a train once and finding an empty carriage. It was an unheard of thing, but I was very tired, so I lay down and fell asleep. With air raids and food shortages, most of us were tired all the time. The first thing I saw when I opened my eyes was a revolver, on the hip of a man, standing over me. There were two men, American servicemen, and one of them said, 'Sorry, ma'am, this carriage is reserved.' But the other one said, 'Well, there's only the two of us. She's not doing any harm.' I said to the first man, 'Listen to him, will you.' So we sat talking all the rest of the way. They were from a big American airbase. The kind airman's name was Felix. I told them that the next time I got home my little girl would be three. Felix said, 'Will she have a party?' I said, 'Of course!' Because you always managed something, however little there was. He said, 'What sort of things does she like?' I said, 'Well, her very favourite thing is fruit salad, but I doubt I'll be able to get that.' Jan loved it. The following week, a seven-pound tin of cubed fruit salad was

delivered to the stage door, courtesy of our
American allies! We opened it for the party, and
the kids thought it was Christmas.

I had a few close shaves. I was in my digs in
Perivale when the first doodlebug dropped.
And I was at the Vaudeville, in *No Medals*, when
a bomb was dropped at the other side of the
Savoy. The whole stage shook. Frederick Leicester,
who was starring with Fay Compton, was on
stage with me when it happened. The audience
started to run out of the theatre – to get to the
shelters. I was playing the cockney maid, and
I looked at Frederick Leicester and I said, in
character, 'Was that somebody at the door?' And
everybody laughed, and quite a few came back
and sat down.

Thorold Dickinson was walking me to the tube
one night, after I'd spent the evening having
dinner with him and his wife, when one of the
V1s came down. There was a big pink flash, and
it knocked us both down on the ground – with
surprise as much as anything. The whole world
went pink for a second.

The only other close shave I had was when Jimmy was based at Aylesbury, and was able to come to London for a few hours in the afternoon. He said, 'I'll meet you under the clock at Piccadilly underground.' He knew that I would be coming from the Strand, because I was calling in to the office of Linnit and Dunfee, the theatrical agents who looked after me in those days.

That afternoon, while I was in their office, a bomb dropped near the Strand Hotel. We all nearly jumped out of our skins. It was very frightening. I went to the Piccadilly tube to meet Jimmy – and it was his face, as he came up the escalator – wondering whether I'd been caught in it. You never knew, in those days, when you were going to lose someone.

Chapter Sixteen
Old Theatricals

You really are talking ancient history if you talk
about music hall. Even in my day, we didn't talk
of music hall. There was the legitimate theatre,
which was acting, and there was variety – a
sequence of acts. Even variety has almost
completely gone now, and I'm sorry for it. At
an evening at a variety theatre, you got a bit of
everything. If you were a variety artist, like my old
television partner on *Meet the Wife*, Freddie
Frinton, you might be in the Broadhead Circuit,
a very good variety chain, and you would get a
touring engagement with them of so many weeks,
doing the same eleven minute turn, twice nightly.

I used to enjoy variety – a bit of conjuring, a bit
of singing and dancing, a bit of comedy. A very
good night out. From the curtain raiser – the poor

bloke who went on first, to get the audience settled down – until the main attraction, the top of the bill, who would usually be the last act, you would get every kind of turn. There was Leyton and Johnson, a famous piano and singer act, who didn't ever speak to each other, apart from during the act. They could earn a thousand pounds a week. Florrie Ford. George Formby. Renee Houston and her sister, Billy, had a singing act. Percy Honri was a concertina player, very well known when I was a kid, and now his grandson works at the BBC. He had a clever billing: A Concert In A Turn (a concertina turn – you see?)

Jimmy was a variety drummer. He came to Morecambe as resident drummer at the Winter Gardens. Broadhead Variety had sold the Winter Gardens to some Morecambe business men, who had it refurbished, new velvet, new gilt, and hired a resident sixteen-piece orchestra, Cecil Hodgkinson and his Harmonics, in which Scottie was the drummer. The town nearly went mad for them. The variety show started at 7.30, and most people were in their seats by seven to listen to the band, they were so good.

After the war, when Scottie was demobbed, the drummer who had taken his place in the Winter Garden's Variety Orchestra while he was in the RAF, said, 'You'll be wanting your old job back, Jimmy.' This was an older fellow with four kids, and Scottie said, 'No, you keep it.' So he came down to London and for a short time he went to work as a clerk in Lyons Bank, at Hammersmith, where the Lyons Corner House offices and storehouse were, just past Olympia. But by this time I was beginning to earn enough money and was getting enough work, to need to have him looking after our accounts and things, and also so one of us could be at home with Jan. I think he must have missed the life of variety at first. His old drum-kit is still downstairs.

Variety artists are entirely different people from 'legit'. Legit – that's another slang term you hardly ever hear used now. Legitimate drama described a body of plays, including Shakespeare, which were considered to be of literary merit, and the idea of 'legitimate theatre' derived from that. A lot of 'legitimate' actors looked down on variety artists, but it was just a kind of snobbery. Good variety artists were often better known, and making a much better living, than many repertory actors.

Although I've worked with many variety artists, I was never in variety. I was always 'legitimate'. When I started out I was a 'character comedienne'. The theatre was my life, for many years. I learned so much about it from my parents. In one play, when I was starting, I had a 'broken' speech – which means some words and then some dots, because another character interrupts you. After he'd seen me on the first night, my father said, 'You know you have that broken speech? Would you please finish the whole sentence for me, that you would have said, if it hadn't been broken.' He made me complete the sentence, and then he got me to say it over and over again, breaking it back a little bit more each time, until I was back to where the speech was broken in the play. It sounds like a waste of time, perhaps, but it completely changed the way I spoke the line. He had been a wonderful director, in his day, my dad. There was always such sensitivity in his productions, about how people actually felt when they were saying something.

Every theatre has its own unique character, its own special smell. Part of it literally is 'the smell of the grease paint'. Men always used cocoa butter to clean off with. My mother rendered down lard and added rose-water and let it set as a base. You put that on under the stage make-up – Leichner number 5 and number 9 – to make it spread on more easily. My mother used to say to me, 'Never forget. The art of make-up is to fool the audience that you really look like that – without make-up.' In the earliest days, if you were dark, you used 'wet white' to look fair-skinned. It was like whitewash. You put a bit in a saucer and then wiped it on with a sponge.

I can see my mother now, expertly putting eye-black on with cotton wrapped round a hairpin, and the blobs were put on after, one on each lash. Very difficult to do. The amateurs all used to say, 'Will you put me some blobs on, Mrs Hird?'

Anyone who has had the privilege and the fun of being a part of it for as long as I have, owes an enormous debt to the theatre, and the thousands of great characters you meet working in it.

I don't know whether they still serve coffee in theatres, but they always used to serve coffee in cups, on trays brought to your seat during the interval, and collected up before the next act. During the war, when I was in *No Medals* at the Vaudeville, one afternoon the trays weren't all collected up and there was a bit of chinking and clinking. Fay Compton, the star, right in the middle of a line, suddenly turned to the audience and said, 'Keep those coffee trays quiet!' It didn't fit in with the play at all, and everyone got such a fright.

The only other time I've experienced anything like that was at the Victoria Palace, when Arthur Askey and I were doing *The Love Match*, and some people in the front row were shelling peanuts and you could hear them, crick, crack. Arthur suddenly turned to them, in the middle of the play, and said, 'When you've finished shelling those peanuts, will you send a few up here?'

Sidney Andrews – by now he will have gone where the good actors go – was the prompt at the Royalty Theatre, Morecambe. He was never on the right page, but it wouldn't have mattered if he had been, because he was never on the right book, either! Last week's script was always sitting on the stool beside him.

A lot of the old comedians were as funny off as they were on stage. It was as though they could not help being funny.

Whenever you worked with Jimmy James, which I had the greatest joy in the world in doing many times, you never sent for any coffee or any tea, because you knew that his entire family were in his dressing room and May, his wife, always had the kettle on the go. His brother Peter, with the wooden leg, dressed him. The one with the Sherlock Holmes cap on was Ely, his nephew, who fell off a chair as a child, and lost an eye.

The only problem with Jimmy was that he couldn't help putting in extra gags. Once when I was doing a television show with him, Jimmy Casey, who was his son, was directing, and every five minutes during rehearsal he was saying, 'Now, Dad, you won't put anything in, will you? It's for television...' And Jimmy James would look hurt and dignified and say, 'Good gracious! Do you think I am not aware of this? This is a very serious piece of work. For *television*. Am I likely to put anything in?'

He is a judge in the first sketch, and I am a JP, wearing a collar and tie, very masculine looking. We have finished rehearsing and are just about to start recording on film. On comes Jimmy Casey, and goes over to his father and speaks to him discreetly but very sternly and Jimmy James is nodding and looking very grave. We could hear him whisper, 'Yes. Yes. I know. I know.'

'Action!' says Jimmy Casey. Jimmy James is the judge. He looks straight across to the clerk of the court and says, 'They're open – do you fancy one?'

'CUT!'

All the way through he was putting bits in – he just couldn't help himself. It was agony... not to laugh, I mean.

Monsewer Eddie Grey was quick. If you passed a broken down old hen house, he would take his cap off and say, 'Oh, I've had some wonderful times there.'

Arthur Askey was once with Monsewer Eddie Grey, on tour, and there was a big case going on in the nearby county court, that had been in the newspapers and everything, so Arthur said to Eddie Grey, 'Let's go in the public gallery and watch a bit of this.' Which they did. And during a recess, one of the ushers came over and said, 'Mr Askey, his lordship saw you were in court and wonders if you would care to join him for a drink in his rooms?' So Arthur goes along, and takes Eddie with him, and introduces him to the judge. While they all have a drink Eddie is very quiet, but he keeps winking at the judge and raising his eyebrows and touching his head, so much so that eventually the judge says to him, 'Is anything the matter, Mr Grey?' And Eddie Grey says, 'I'm sorry, your honour, but I couldn't help wondering, is that a wig you're wearing?'

The judge – who was wearing an enormous curly white judge's wig, practically down to his shoulders – said, 'Well, yes.'

And Eddie said, 'Yes, I thought so... you can see the join!'

A nice thing about doing a season at Blackpool was that a lot of you would meet up and socialize at lunch-time. Everyone was very friendly. We would meet at the Opera House for lunch, at a long oak table, and you took your turns at paying for 'a lunch'. One season, I think it must have been about 1958, Morecambe and Wise were at one theatre, Ken Dodd at another, Tommy Cooper was at the Queen's... it was tremendous. But everyone was forever playing tricks on one another. Charlie Chester, God rest him, had paid for 'a lunch' the day before, and George Black said to each of us, 'When lunch is over, all leave quickly, in ones and twos, and leave Charlie behind to pay again.' You should have seen Charlie Chester's face as we all got up and left him, 'Well, I must be going. See you tomorrow!' Of course, we paid him back later.

At the Victoria Palace, in London, the Crazy Gang – Flanagan and Allen, Naughton and Gold, Nervo and Knox, and, most of the time, Monsewer Eddie Grey – always took time off for holidays one at a time. One August Bank Holiday week I was up in Morecambe doing a play. After rehearsals three of us were having a drink in the cocktail bar of the Crown. (Does anybody talk about the 'cocktail bar' now?) We had just ordered our drinks when someone I knew from the Winter Gardens came in, and seeing me said, 'Hallo,

Thor! How are you, darling? Did you know that
Charlie Naughton is sitting in the Midland Hotel?'

I said, 'He's not!' And that was enough for me
to know that he was the one off, the member of
the Crazy Gang not working for the next week.
I said to the barman, 'Don't serve the drinks.
Remember we've ordered, because we'll be back
later.'

We all went along to the Midland, and I went
straight into the ladies' powder room and said to
the attendant, who knew me very well, 'What have
you come in?'

She said, 'How do you mean?'

I said, 'To come to work in today – what did
you wear?'

She said, 'Just my mac and a scarf.'

I said, 'Good.' And I put them on. I had already
spotted Charlie as I came in, seated at a table with
a white cap on, holding court, surrounded by
about seven hotel guests, all buying him Bass
– empty bottles on the table in front of him,
everybody admiring him. I went up behind him,
wearing the mac and scarf. The people didn't
recognize me, and I said in a trembling voice,

167

'Charlie, give us a couple of quid to get the kids some fish and chips, will you? We're standing waiting at the front there, like you said, and it's so cold... we've been there nearly an hour.'

He never looked round. Out came the wallet. He silently passed back a couple of notes, 'Now shove off!' he said, still not turning round. You should have seen the faces of those visitors!

I returned the mac and scarf to the ladies' room, and we went back to the Crown for the drinks we'd ordered. I was staying at the Clarendon.

When I got back that night, after the performance, they said, 'There have been three calls for you.'

I said, 'All from Mr Naughton?'

'Oh yes! However did you know?'

'Two pounds tells me.'

I loved it in Blackpool when we would give one performance during a season for all the landladies – who had an organization, with a chairman and everything – and afterwards I would have about nine of them round in the dressing room, and they'd all be in their suits with bits of mink on, and there would be all of this, 'Of course, I won't be here for your last night – we're going round the world.' It used to kill me. I used to think, 'Who are you putting it on for, girl?'

On the stairs as you go up in my mews house, are two handles off the dress circle doors at the Royalty Theatre. When they were demolishing the theatre, they asked me if there was anything I'd like as a memento, and I said, 'Yes, I'd like a set of the dress circle door handles.' I never thought how glad I would be to have them, all these years later, to help me get up the stairs when my arthritis is playing me up.

Then I have, on the door on the bottom of the stairs, the Exeter Theatre pass door handle. The door at the top pulls to with a St James's Theatre handle. All lovingly polished.

They were wonderful days in the theatre – I hope they still are for the young people coming in to it these days. I'm sure they are.

Ealing Studios

It was a studio on its own, Ealing. During the war I played a land-girl in *Next of Kin*, with Elizabeth Allen. In another one I was an ATS girl. I remember doing a film about a concentration camp, *Two Thousand Women*, with Renee Houston. Two hundred women trying to look like two thousand in a prison camp. Jan and Vera, her nanny, were down in London for a long weekend, and there were so many sirens and bomb alerts going, I told them to come to the studios. I said to Vera, 'If we're going to be killed, we'll all be killed together.'

During rehearsals Jan, aged four, hair in plaits, wearing a pair of check trousers, carrying her little Tatchy Case, as she called it, with a few toys in, was found wandering about and 'discovered' by the director, and was given a part in the film!

I went to Ealing last year, to do a little interview with Harry Secombe for *Songs of Praise*, together with Kathy Staff and Bill Owen. There were only two stages at Ealing in the old days. I had a little walk round on my own, and I went into

Wardrobe, and I looked at the walls, which were the old, original walls, and I said, 'This used to be Make-up, didn't it, in the old days?' They said, 'Yes, it did. Fancy you knowing that.'

I said, 'I was made up in this room, for my very first screen test.'

EXPERIENCED ACTOR, pupil of Miss Rosina Filippi, and late of the 'Court' Theatre, 'St Martin's' Theatre, 'Compton Comedy Co.' etc., gives lessons to a limited number of pupils, in Elocution, Diction, Interpretation. Plays produced for amateurs. Suburbs visited. Reply ANATOLE JAMES, 24, Oxford Terrace, Hyde Park, W. 2

The Magic Circle

A new society for the
elevation and protection
of the Art of Magic.
Offices: St. George's Hall, W.

To the Ladies of the Audience

In England, the privilege of being able to leave the auditorium, and find an enjoyable corner in which to enjoy a cigarette, a cup of coffee, or some favourite beverage, has been generally monopolised by the male portion of the audience; and little has been done up to the present to change a practice more in keeping with the Victorian period than our own times.

The old-fashioned notion of keeping the sexes apart in drawing room and smoking room is now discarded in the best hotels and steamships. Lounges where men and women may sit together are substituted, with approval from everybody.

The Management of the Savoy Theatre would, therefore, draw the attention of their lady patrons to the fact that the saloons of the theatre have been made thoroughly attractive and prepared for their reception. The Stalls and the Dress Circle have been decorated by the eminent Australian artist, Mr James Quinn, R.I.B.A., whilst those attached to the other parts of the theatre will be found exceptionally comfortable and inviting.

Chapter Seventeen

'A Penny For Going'

I've always liked to think of myself as a good business woman. One of my father's sayings was, 'If you work for nowt, you're worth nowt.' So if Neville or I, even as kids, did a good job, we got paid something, even if it was only a penny.

My father was manager when they put on a production of *Il Trovatore*, in the days when John Riding's Opera Company used to come to Morecambe pier theatre each year for a summer season. Part of the scenery was a rock that the hero hides behind, but the brace and bit to hold the rock in place was missing. My dad said to Neville, 'Get behind that rock, will you, and hold it still.' He had to lie there, not moving, for a whole act, and it was a bit crowded when the tenor was hiding behind the rock as well! But at

the end of the week Neville got a little fawn wage
envelope with a half crown in it, and on the
outside it said, 'Neville Hird – Assistant Property
Master'. After my mother died, I found it in
her jewel box, and the half crown was still in
the envelope.

For a small wage, I sold programmes in the
theatre that were perfumed with a scent called
Amo-del. We got a whole pile of programmes and
an enamel bowl with Amo-del in it, and we sat
them in it. Then I wafted through the auditorium
waving them, saying, 'Programmes! Threepence
each!' And people would sniff and say, 'Ooh, this
is nice. Thank you.' It said on them, 'This
programme is perfumed with Amo-del.'

The fire-sheet had to come down once in the
evening, that is the law, to show that if there is a
fire back-stage, it cannot reach the audience.
Theatre fire-sheets were always covered in
advertisements, like 'Dr Williams's Pink Pills for
Pale People'. Or 'Don't wear a truss – go to
Slaters!' (I don't know what happened to you
at Slaters!)

In Morecambe, in the Pier Theatre, the fire curtain was entirely taken up by John Birkett, with his Amo-del perfume. There was a canoe with an Indian in it, red flowers all flowing back into the lake, purple mountains in the background, and it said: 'Amo-del – the gathered fragrance of Indian dales'. I thought it was so clever and beautiful.

The proscenium arch was as big as Drury Lane's. It was vast. On the other side of the stage from the pass door (which you go through at your peril, without permission, because it leads to the 'pretend' side of the theatre, the stage area) was another door, with a hatch, and a shutter which went up and down. Through that came trays of jellies for the interval. They were threepence each, in a little dish with a spoon, and ice-cream round them, provided by the two Miss Hintons, who had the cafe on the pier, where a nice big cup of coffee, or Horlicks, was threepence.

The jellies came in different colours, red, yellow and green. On any night when the attendant wasn't available, my father would say to Nev and me, 'Now one of you two – well, both of you, take the jelly trays round in the interval.' He'd give us twopence wages. Once the fire-sheet started going up, you knew you wouldn't sell any more, so you collected up the trays and took them through to the back. If there were less than four dishes left, we were allowed to eat them. On one occasion there were two left. Our Nev says, 'Good oh!' A teaspoon took half of the jelly. We had just had a teaspoonful each, so two halves had gone, when there was a knock on the hatch and a call, 'One more jelly, please!' In a flash Nev stuck our two halves of jelly together on one plate, stuck a bit of ice-cream over the top to hide the join, and pushed it through the hatch. It was so quick I was still poised to take my second mouthful. I said, 'But we'd half eaten...' He said, 'It was all on there for threepence.' I thought, 'What a business man!'

Cheapside was parallel with Euston Road, which was our shopping street, although when I see it now, it seems so small... That meant that the back street, the passage between the back gates, were shared by Euston Road one side, and us on the other. Our back door faced the back of 33 Euston Road, which was Spencer's Cafe, run by my

'auntie' Molly and 'auntie' Martha – no relation
but I always called them auntie. They had a
bathroom and we didn't, so we always went there
for a bath. The 'cafe' was really just their upstairs
front room, where they served dinners for
workmen. They asked me to be a waitress for one
day. I was thrilled. Anything that meant acting
being what I wasn't, I enjoyed. So I served the
men their mince and potatoes and rice pudding.
They gave me a shilling – but like I've said, you
were 'in the money' with a shilling.

We used to go to Gibson's for the bread. They
were awfully smart, the Miss Gibsons. I don't
know why we thought their shop window was so
posh, now I come to think of it. It was only a vase
of flowers, a few loaves and some oven bottom
cakes arranged on green tiles. When you were
baking, the bit of dough that was left, too small
for a loaf tin, went in the bottom of the oven, and
that was why they are called 'oven bottom cakes'.
Oh, and they tasted good when they were still
warm, with home-made jam on. You can still
get them in the north of England, oven bottom
cakes.

Like a lot of confectioners in those days, the Gibsons would bake your own loaves for you. My mother often used to say to me, 'Will you go for Mrs Rhodes' bread...' or 'Mrs Baynes' bread', or 'Mrs Houghton's bread'. Most women with large families made their own bread, their own two pound loaves, but if you didn't have an oven large enough for five two pound loaves of bread, you took your tins of dough along to your local baker's or confectioner's, where they would put them into their large oven for you and bake them, for a few coppers. I suppose the term 'baker' came from that – it was where they baked the bread for the community. I can remember in back Peddar Street they had one department that was only for local people's bread. Can you imagine, now, if you went into your local supermarket and said, 'Excuse me, just put these five loaves in your oven for me, would you? I'll be back about five o'clock.'

As I say, I like to think of myself as a business woman, and I used to go to Gibson's to collect people's bread that had been baked, and my mother would always say, 'And don't you take anything...' But you see, if you're a business woman, that's not right, is it? Mrs Rhodes would say, 'Here you are, love, here's a penny for going.' That's when the acting prowess came into it, because I had to say virtuously, 'Oh no thank you. It's all right, Mrs Rhodes,' but oh, how I would look at that penny in her hand so wistfully...

I now have neighbours who go shopping for me. Donald Across gets me things like paper tissues and kitchen roll. Bob Next-door-but-one brings me milk and bread every other day, and my newspaper every day. George Next-door-but-two always has a hammer ready if I need anything.

Whenever they bring me anything, I always give them 'a penny for going'. I keep pennies especially for them, in my purse. It made them laugh the first time, and they said they didn't want anything, but I said, 'Yes you do! If you knew the agony I went through, with Mrs Rhodes and Mrs Baynes, saying "No thank you, I don't want anything!"' So now they know they're going to get 'a penny for going' and they take it to please me.

Some people of my age say, 'Oh, things were better in the good old days.' All I can say is that all my days have been happy and loving since the day I was born. I've loved every minute of my life, and am still loving it. At 87, what could be better than that?

AFTERNOON TEA

A special service of TEA (freshly made for each order) is served at Matinees in the Saloons and in the Auditorium

6d.

TO FACILITATE SERVICE VISITORS ARE KINDLY REQUESTED TO ORDER IN ADVANCE

'The Friend of my Youth'

GIBSON'S

Old Fashioned

Treacle Toffee & Cream Toffee

In 6d. TINS   In 3d. PKTS

Very Delicious Sweetmeats.
Can be had from the Attendants.

Word List

78 rpm records
AA rider on motorbike
antimacassars
a penny for going
aspidistras
Assistant Property
   Master
bacon slicer
ballroom dancing and
   drinking Horlicks
bandstand
barrels of butter
Bath-chair
battledore and
   shuttlecock
bentwood cane-bottom

chairs
billeting office
black lead
black out curtains
boiling shrimps in the
   back yards
borax
bowlers
box of Fleetwood
   kippers
brass weights
Broadhead Circuit –
   variety chain
brown paper parcels of
   'towels'
brown paper vests

butcher's basket
Button A and Button B
camphor bags
camphor blocks
candlesticks
candlestick telephones
canteen of cutlery
carbolic soap
careless talk costs lives
carpet beating
chair cane mender
character comedienne
checks and gumsheets
chilblains
Christmas tree candles
clicking
clothes horse
clothes prop
clothes rack
coal-holes
coal scuttle
cobbler/shoemaker's
    iron last
cobbling, tiling and

thatching
cocktail bar
cocoa butter greasepaint
coffee trays in the
    interval
coloured curl pins
colour wash
combs/combinations
confectioners who bake
    customers' own bread
Co-op divi (dividend)
copper boiler
coppers
Cornish frill
costume
courting
crash gear boxes
cream soda
crimps
cross-over dress
cruet
curtain raiser
cut apples
cycle shop

dancing outside on the
   pier
darning needles
dickey-seat
dig for victory
distemper
District Nurse
'doing the mincemeat'
'doing the raisins'
doing your bit
dolly pegs
dolly-stick
dolly-tub
Don't you know there's a
   war on?
doodlebugs
driving gloves
earphone plaits
egg and spoon races
eleven minute turn
evening Chapel
fender
Fielden Wood System
fire-sheet

fish and two
fish-cart
fishing families
flat-iron
flintstone walls
flitch bacon
flukes
fly cemetery/fly papers
follow my leader
ganzies
gas lamps
gas mantles
gas masks
going out regular
goose grease
gozunder
grating suet
guard's van
half a crown
Halt/whistle stops
hand-carts
hand-tied bow tie
hat pins
hiking

hobs
hopscotch
horsehair sofa
horse trams
hot pea sellers
hound trail
Hudson's dried soap
   powder
'If I'm spared!'
If you work for nowt,
   you're worth nowt
ironing sheet
Is your journey really
   necessary?
Izal
jelly and ice-cream in a
   paper case
joy
killing yourself with
   kindness
knife and fork tea
knife-grinder
knitted dishcloths
knockers up

'Ladies only'
   compartments
lamp lighter
lamp oil
lard and rose-water
   grease paint
leather straps on train
   windows
legitimate stage
Leichner numbers
   5 and 9
liberty bodice
like silly devils
lime block
limelight
lime perch
limestone
Lobby Ludd
longjohns
lying in
Lyons Corner House
make do and mend
mangle
manned signal boxes

'May I have the pleasure
   of this dance?'
Meccano sets
men's outfitting
milk-carts
milk-churns
mincemeat Sunday
mob cap
modesty vests
Morecambe Bay Potted
   Shrimps
muffin man
mullinger of shrimps
Music Hall
muslin lavender bag
napkin rings
net luggage racks
News Chronicle
night soil men
oil of almonds and
   essence of violets
onion boxes
orange crates
oven bottom cakes

pairs of kippers
Palace of Varieties
pantry
pass door
patent leather and kid
   buttoned boots
Pearl White
pea-souper fogs
pegging a rug
pestle and mortar sign
Petty
picking shrimps
picking table
pikelets
pink pills for pale people
Pip, Squeak and Wilfred
   club
'Pitch... patch... pepper'
plaited raffia skipping
   ropes
playing in the street
playing shop
playmates
plus fours/plus twos

pneumatic suction
   system
posser
possing
poss-tub
Postman's knock
pound note
'Press Button A' and
   'Press Button B'
privy
rag-and-bone man
ration books
ribbon paper
rough shrimps
sack races
Saturday morning
   cinema
'Saw' balls
school gym slip
school slate
scullery
seaside landladies
sea trader on the high
   seas

sheet music
Shemin nessim
shilling in the pound
   and a twopenny
   bonus
shirt studs
shroud
silver threepenny bits
sing-song
sixpenny records from
   Woolworth's
skiffle groups
smell of the greasepaint
spats
spiffy box (box of stylish
   things, like brass tie
   pins!)
spills and tapers
spi's ball
spot dances
stage trunk
steam-cleaning van
steam trains
steel gramophone

needles
stone hot-water bottles
stone jars
'suitable to the waters of
   the district'
Sunday best
Sunday night cinema
tailor's marking chalk
talking politics round
   the lamp
tartan travelling rug
tea-set
telegrams
telephone operator
ten-shilling note
terry towelling nappies
the duration
tie-pins
toasting fork
toilet set
toll calls
top of the bill
trams and trolley buses
tram tickets

treasure chest
troop trains
trunk calls
truss
twin-tub washing
   machine
twist of tea
two-pound loaf for
   fourpence halfpenny
V1 and V2
valance
Variety artists/turns
walking out
wallpaper windmills
waltzing
wash-board
washing set
water closet
watercress man
wearing a hat at home
wedding telegrams
Wef breakfast, Wef
   supper, Wef tea
wet white

wheel tapper
whip and top
whisky all in
window tappers
wind-up gramophone
wireless accumulator
wireless shop
wooden skewers
woodyard

working man's enamel
can
worm cakes
wounded soldiers
yellow-stone
your intended
'Your time's up, caller'
Zebo